"This truly remarkable book [...] e high price and higher privilege of being [...] ature known to man: obeying the next thing God [...] irit's enablement. If you yearn for a deeper understanding of God's character and His ways, then *Epic Faith* will certainly help to get you there. Marty tells it like it is, in his transparent un-whitewashed style, coming from his and Kelly's numerous personal sagas. Warning: This book is not for wimps! I give it my highest recommendation."

JOY DAWSON
International Bible teacher and author

"As a leader in YWAM, Marty has practiced our 'do first, then teach' value. Marty has been practicing epic faith for years; now through this book he is teaching others to do so. We need more books like this not only to inspire but to teach how important it is to listen to Jesus and obey him in all details."

LOREN CUNNINGHAM
Cofounder, Youth With A Mission

"I would like to commend Marty Meyer to you as a man of faith, who leans into God's Word, listens for His guiding Voice, and obeys, trusting in His Character. Marty shares my commitment to walk a faith-filled life, based on God's faithfulness to us, and to search out young people with leadership potential to help lead the Church in the decades to come. *Epic Faith* is a very personal and practical book, filled with wonderful stories of God proving His faithfulness to us when we step out in obedience to Him."

DARLENE CUNNINGHAM
Cofounder, Youth With A Mission

"Marty has written a gripping, thrilling, and refreshing account of what a life of faith looks like when a life is fully surrendered to Jesus. The stories are incredible and give much glory to God. Marty has managed to masterfully lace together exciting storytelling of his journey with God intermingled with scripture, sound teaching, and wise counsel about living a life of faith. You'll not get through this book without being utterly challenged and inspired by the Holy Spirit to live your own life of faith and fulfill the High Calling of God; nor will you get through it with dry eyes. This is one of the most informative, encouraging, and uplifting books I've ever read, a *must* read for all ages."

KEL STEINER
Director of YWAM Myrtle Beach; author of Adventures in Saying Yes to God

"The word *faith* often refers to ones religion or system of beliefs. For my friend Marty Meyer it is a Bible-based, experienced life journey. This personal, unique story is can't-put-it-down exciting because it is a proven faith of lived-out reality where God is often the only possible explanation."

DEAN SHERMAN
Author and international Bible teacher

"Marty Meyer has written a remarkable book. As you read it you discover that it is like sitting on a porch with a friend recounting poignant lessons he has learned. In a graceful, winsome way, he conveys deep truths of the kingdom of God that motivates the reader to say yes to God for whatever next step He is calling for in their life."

BISHOP BILL ATWOOD
Dean of international affairs, The Anglican Church in North America

"Marty Meyer takes us through his journey in following God and gives us practical stories that will challenge you to go deeper with God whether you are a new believer or a tried and true saint. Marty is honest in sharing his fears and unbelief as he stepped out on the water to follow Jesus and how God continued to grow him in being a man marked with epic faith."

REV. DR. TIM SVOBODA
YWAM International Cities Coordinator

"God writes his story in the lives of people throughout the Bible. He does the same today. In *Epic Faith* Marty tells his story, but he demonstrates it is more about God's story than it is about his own. Get ready to be challenged and opened to how God is inviting you into his mission! Get ready to discover your own epic faith!"

DR. ROGER THEIMER
Executive pastor, King of Kings Church, Omaha, Nebraska;
founder and director, Kids Kount Publishing

"Marty Meyer is a dynamic leader who has helped mobilize thousands of high school youth through our YWAM Mission Adventures program. I first met Marty in 1989 when he joined a small outreach team that went around the world. Marty is a leader who hears from God, obeys God, and trusts God even when the circumstances look impossible. Marty is a leader that embodies *Epic Faith.*"

SEAN LAMBERT
International founder of Homes of Hope and Mission Adventures

"*Epic Faith* is one of the most impacting books I have ever read. This book wrecked my heart again and again as tears streamed down my face. If you are a young Christian, *Epic Faith* will put a fire in your heart, build great faith, and give you a desire to live for God. If you have served God for many years and have become weary, Epic Faith will deeply impact you, calling you into new intimacy and bringing renewed life in Christ."

WICK NEASE
Founder and director, Streams of Mercy

"People tend to follow leaders who inspire them. Marty's personal journey with the word of God, the voice of God, and the character of God, will motivate growth toward greater faith, devotion, and personal connection with Jesus. Refresh your faith—read this book!"

DOUG HEZELTINE
Lead pastor, Christian Life Fellowship, Ontario, Oregon;
publishing consultant, Good Catch Publishing

"From the moment I met Marty and Kelly Meyer in their Discipleship Training School, God spoke to my heart that they were a powerful couple with destiny written all over them. My wife and I have had the privilege of being their close friends and having a front seat watching them grow into giants of the faith. Through a near deadly train crash, salvation, commitment, rejection, trust, pain, frustration, depression and periods of suffering and triumph, you will sit on the edge of your seat watching their epic faith."

DAVE GUSTAVESON
Director, Global Target Network, Youth With A Mission

"Great read! *Epic Faith* is very engaging, challenging, inspiring, and practical. It will challenge and inspire you to a greater walk of faith, and give you practical steps of how to cultivate it. This is not theoretical; Marty humbly shares with incredible transparency his own journey of faith. Having known him for over twenty-five years I can tell you this is the real deal!"

ROD ENOS
Pastor, Southside Christian Center, Boise, Idaho

"Marty's stories are full of intrigue, adventure, raw faith and miracles, and best of all they are all true! If you have a radical love for Jesus, you will not be able to put this book down!"

PETER ILIYN
Former North American director of Youth With A Mission

"*Epic Faith* reminds us that with God, nothing is impossible! Marty's transparency and vivid detail had me hanging on every word. This book stirred up something inside of me that increased my own personal faith by reminding me that God is still in the miracle-working business. *Epic Faith* will remind the reader that God loves us and cares deeply about every detail in our life."

JIM DURAN
Lead pastor, The River Community Church, Ventura, California

"If your faith walk has become stagnant, then you need to read *Epic Faith*. You will be inspired to grow your own faith, which will allow you to accomplish great things for God's kingdom through your life."

TIM VALENTINE
President/CEO, Jeremiah 29:11 Inc.

"I have invited Marty to speak, and every time he opens his mouth I find myself inspired to be more loving, more resolute in seeking God, and more willing to trust Him. This book is no different. We hear stories of people who have trusted God and been used by Him to do amazing things, but Marty challenges us to actually live in that story line. Through this book Marty's voice is resonating, prompting, and inspiring us to be willing to do anything for Christ."

ALLEN BARTIMIOLI
Mission and outreach pastor, Faith Bible Church, Phoenix, Arizona

"'Without faith, you cannot please God.' Marty clearly outlines that real, epic faith is actually a lived-out and fulfilling relationship with the living God. The stories Marty shares are his own, but the truths contained in them are powerful, eternal. His testimonies will reach into your heart and encourage you to write your own story of Epic Faith. I have known Marty for many years. He is as real as it gets. The richness of his faith is attested by those closest to him. Sharing vulnerably, Marty illustrates through his own life that a life lived with lesser lovers is bound to disappoint, but that a life lived encountering the living God is destined to fulfill. As you journey with Marty through the pages of his life, you will meet the source of all change, of all things eternal. I encourage you to read and reflect on his story. It is a testimony of someone who did not settle for lesser lovers, but responded to the greatest lover of all, and there, he found both power and peace."

JEREMIAH SWEEP
Missionary, South Asia

EPIC
FAITH

Rooted in the Word, Voice, and Character of God

MARTY MEYER

YWAM PUBLISHING
Seattle, Washington

YWAM Publishing is the publishing ministry of Youth With A Mission (YWAM), an international missionary organization of Christians from many denominations dedicated to presenting Jesus Christ to this generation. To this end, YWAM has focused its efforts in three main areas: (1) training and equipping believers for their part in fulfilling the Great Commission (Matthew 28:19), (2) personal evangelism, and (3) mercy ministry (medical and relief work).

For a free catalog of books and materials, call (425) 771-1153 or (800) 922-2143. Visit us online at www.ywampublishing.com.

Epic Faith: Rooted in the Word, Voice, and Character of God
Copyright © 2016 by Marty Meyer

Published by YWAM Publishing
a ministry of Youth With A Mission
P.O. Box 55787, Seattle, WA 98155-0787

Library of Congress Cataloging-in-Publication Data is on file at the Library of Congress.

ISBN 978-1-57658-933-5

Some names and identifying information have been changed to protect the privacy of individuals.

Cover photograph: "Chapel of Light" by Andrew Waddington. Used by permission.

First printing 2016

Printed in the United States of America

This book is dedicated to Kelly, my wife, best friend, and love of my life. God knew what he was doing to bless me with a gal spicy enough to join me in this epic journey and to do so with such grace, wisdom, and resilience. It is with good reason that her picture permanently serves as a bookmark to Proverbs 31 in my well-worn study Bible—as she is truly a remarkable woman of faith.

Kelly, thank you for saying yes to me over twenty-five years ago and for following Jesus together with me every day since! I love you.

The cover photograph, "Chapel of Light," is used with the permission of freelance photographer Andrew Waddington. I was immediately drawn to this image for its powerful statement of rugged beauty. It speaks to the truths that I convey in this book, that true faith is rooted in the rock-solid foundation of God's Word, his voice, and his unchanging character. Abundant life grows out of and thrives within the protection of God's presence.

I first met Andrew while camping with my family in southern Utah near Monument Valley. We struck up a conversation with this eccentric photographer while mutually waiting for our laundry at the campground facility. Kelly invited him to join us in our vintage camper for walnut pancakes, fried eggs, and orange juice, and we instantly grew to appreciate the depth of Andrew's personality. We prayed for the success of his photo shoots, and after spending several days and several more breakfasts together, Kelly gave Andrew her compact Bible.

Andrew spends most of his time traveling the globe, capturing stunning images like this one. His photography skill and eye for beauty are obvious. By visiting andrewwaddington.com you can admire more of Mr. Waddington's exceptional work.

We feel blessed to know Andrew and are privileged to use his masterful photograph for the cover of this book.

Contents

Foreword

I FIRST met Marty and Kelly Meyer shortly after they accepted an invitation to lead the Mission Adventures program at Youth With A Mission in Los Angeles over twenty years ago. I was able to observe them growing in their own "epic faith" up close and personal as I would visit that campus to teach at least twice a year during their tenure there. Since their move to Idaho our personal times have been fewer and farther between, but I have kept abreast of their ventures in faith in the area of world missions.

Epic Faith looks from the outset like a simple three-point message on faith that any preacher could come up with. This autobiographical sketch of their lives, however, is no such treatment of faith as a theoretical concept; it is a raw account of a sometimes not-so-epic faith as they grew in obedience to the next thing God told them to do. It is filled with honesty and the emotional ups and downs of living a life of faith and understanding both the wisdom and revelation (Eph. 1:17) it takes to live a life trusting in God's Word, Voice, and Character. Marty's balanced, biblical treatment of issues—controversial in some sectors—is broken down into twenty-six chapters, with simple exhortations delivered via teaching and story.

Epic Faith is about a young couple willing to suffer the rejection of their peers and misunderstandings of others to pursue God's dream for them. It is a fast-moving tale of the Supernatural working through natural people. As you read the following pages, your faith will be stirred as you not only focus on the story but also apply helpful principles to your own journey.

Danny Lehmann
International Dean, College of Christian Ministries, University of the Nations
Honolulu, Hawaii

Acknowledgments

A L L glory to my Lord and Savior, Jesus Christ, who is forever my friend and King in this epic life journey! May you be lifted high.

Deep appreciation goes to my friend and brother-in-law, Chard Berndt, who invested countless hours editing the manuscript before it was ever sent to the publisher. The final product not only reflects his excellent writing skills but testifies to his own commitment and dedication to this project. Thank you, Chard, for a job well done and for decades of mountain peak climbing and adventures!

My wife, Kelly, also pored over the manuscript and her passion for word-crafting added vibrancy to this epic story. Thank you for determining to tell the story well!

I have two of the greatest teens on the planet. They were quick to ask about my progress and always ready to dish out encouragement. Isaac and Sadie, you are my gifts!

I appreciate my good and faithful friend Wayne Shauan, who contributed his graphic art talent to this project. He shows up on many pages of this book and for good reason—his friendship has deeply impacted my life. Thanks for being my cohort in countless epic mountain bike exploits over the years.

Tom Bragg, Ryan Davis, Warren Walsh, and the entire team at YWAM Publishing have been a joy to work with. Over the years Tom has prodded my authorship, frequently asking, "When are you going to write your book?" His encouragement gave me the confidence to go for it. YWAM Publishing's commitment to excellence is combined with their love for people, making them unique and personal in their field. I'm grateful for their careful treatment of my manuscript and bringing it to completion as a quality piece of work.

I spent years learning many faith lessons from my parents, Bob and Milly Meyer, simply by observing their poured-out lives of servanthood and generosity. I'm so glad you get to be home with Jesus, but we all still miss you. I am deeply grateful for my siblings, Rob, Julie, and Carrie, who have been anchors in my life, supporting one another's journeys through mutual love and respect.

I owe a debt of gratitude to the vast number of godly heroes who have invested in my life—both named and unnamed in this book. Thank you!

I want to thank our entire YWAM Idaho team for their prayers, support, and understanding throughout this Epic Faith process. You are an amazing team.

Introduction

Now faith is the substance of things hoped
for, the evidence of things not seen.
HEBREWS 11:1 NKJV

I AM inviting you into my story: an extremely personal narrative, in raw emotion, of my quest to discover God and unabashedly follow him. Through this process, God has taught me to lift my eyes above my circumstances in order to see him through every event. I have enjoyed seasons of pure joy and have tasted the bitterness of suffering. The following chapters relay my journey, through which God has schooled me in the subject of epic faith. I share my story in hopes that it will inspire you to attain a faith firmly focused on God.

In the following narrative, I'll share keys of faith so simple they tend to get missed. Before we launch into any epic tales, however, a few thoughts will make our journey more productive:

It is not the size of our faith but the focus of our faith that makes the difference.

Many believers fall exhausted and disillusioned by a misguided notion of self-focused faith: "If I just pray hard enough, if I really believe, if I just have enough faith, then God will answer my prayers." I call this self-directed approach "faith in faith." Such faith will never be enough, as it ultimately looks to our limited selves.

Perhaps the disciples had adopted this idea when they asked Jesus in Matthew 17, "Why couldn't we drive out the demon and heal the boy?"

Jesus gave a puzzling explanation. He responded that it was "because you have so little faith" but then proceeded to tell them that they needed only faith the size of a mustard seed—about the smallest thing one can imagine. I think Jesus wants us to comprehend that it is not the amount or size of our faith that matters but the size of our God. Jesus wants us to focus our faith on him.

A few of these disciples had recently descended from the mountain where Jesus had revealed himself in glory. They had heard the audible voice of the Father declaring that Jesus was the Son of God. Where else, or on whom else, should our faith ever be focused? Rather than a benign notion of faith misdirected toward oneself, we must explore the epic faith that focuses on God.

Our faith is focused on God alone.

We need to stop over-examining ourselves and sizing up our problems, and instead direct our gaze to the Almighty One. The focus of our faith is the glorious Son of God, the Creator of the universe, the Author of life, the Redeemer and Savior, the living Lord Jesus Christ. Nothing is impossible for him. And nothing will be impossible for you and me when we focus on God to accomplish his purposes through his strength.

This book is sectioned into three emphases: the Word of God, the Voice of God, and the Character of God. I have determined these to be major movements in the symphony of my life, through which Jesus has relayed important aspects of God-focused faith. He has used experiences in each movement to redirect my focus from self to him. I have come to appreciate the simple truth that he has walked alongside me every single step of my way, and I enthusiastically invite you into my journey.

God-focused faith is based on his Word.

When younger, I came to know Jesus personally by reading the Bible. The inerrant, infallible, inspired Word of God is the foundation of our faith because it reveals who God is and how he relates to us. His Word can always be trusted.

God-focused faith is based on his voice.

Later, I learned to discern and follow the voice of God. Faith in him is dynamic, relational, and intimate. Through his voice, we learn of God's living and active presence in our days, and he compels us to follow his individualized leading in our lives.

God-focused faith is based on his character.

Through major life transitions, God has taught me to base my faith on his character. As we experience God in our lives intimately, we come to know him more thoroughly. Our faith is not resting on merely knowing facts *about God*, but on actually *knowing God*—his ways and his character. God is our Father and he treasures our deeper knowledge of him. The more completely we know him, the more our faith will actively be built on trusting his never-changing character.

Faith that is focused on God is inherently epic.

An epic is a long narrative poem or story that includes a hero. The hero of God's story is Jesus, and he invites us into his narrative by faith. When we come to the cross of Christ, our story dramatically changes and becomes pregnant with epic potential. Our lives become a beautiful tale of transformation, renewal, goodness, life, and profound love. With Jesus as the central hero, our story will glorify God and reflect his character. The plot of a life fully surrendered to and focused on God reflects a passionate pursuit of his dreams for us.

Epic faith accomplishes great things with God.

God is calling men and women today to choose to live epic faith. In response to this call, we will do great things for him as we walk with him. Epic faith is not rooted in our limited human strength but rather in our unshakable confidence that stems from knowing our limitless God.

The heroes of faith described in Hebrews 11 inspire me. A simple study of their lives reveals ordinary people who accomplished extraordinary feats because they knew God and followed him. Clearly, these men and women displayed a unique perspective, one that values eternity, obedience, and pointing others to the Father. Their lives were marked by hardship and trial that shaped their faith and its focus. God desires to refine our faith, even using difficulty, so we can fully embody his great plans.

Lives of epic faith are fulfilling.

Epic faith can revive lost dreams and provide confidence that all things are possible for the one who believes. God has planted dream seeds in your heart, and in the following pages you will find courage to trust the One who can nourish those dreams into life. A God-sized dream is one that you cannot achieve in your own strength or with your own power. It will ultimately bring glory to God when he accomplishes it through you. My prayer is that you will discover—and enjoy—the epic faith journey that God intends for you.

Before we begin, I challenge you to apply these principles within your own prayer life. Create a prayer list by identifying some needs that you want Jesus to address. To assist in this process, download the free "Epic Prayer List" template available at www.epicfaith.net. This practical resource will help you powerfully integrate the Word, Voice, and Character of God into your prayer life. You can also order *30 Days of Epic Faith*, available at www.epicfaith.net. This companion workbook details the scriptural foundation to *Epic Faith*. It's formatted as a thirty-day spiritual fitness program that is like rocket fuel for your faith.

Finally, as you begin to walk through these pages, I want you to be aware that when God looks at you, he sees an epic hero of faith in the making. Brace yourself for an adventure!

PART ONE

The Word of God

Jesus, the Son of God, walked out of the pages of the Bible and became as real to me as any person I knew in this world.

ONE

Golden Idols

A SUNNY spring afternoon emerged as the tires of my glittering gold Toyota Corolla rolled over the rain-soaked roads of my hometown in Winfield, Kansas. Another thunderstorm had passed through, delivering sheets of rain, and my friend Matt and I were headed to Tunnel Mill Dam to watch giant trees crash over it as the Walnut River ran at flood stage. As usual, my Pioneer stereo pumped out classics from my favorite groups—Lynyrd Skynyrd, Boston, and Rush. The metallic car that showcased these tunes was my life as a high school junior. I had sunk all of my savings into it, adding a custom steering wheel, stereo system, and chrome wheels. It reigned as the vehicle of choice for dragging Main Street with my buddies.

I had attended Christian school since kindergarten, memorizing Bible verses and participating in catechism classes. My family went to church every Sunday, and I knew all about God and the Bible: more than enough religion, I thought. I figured my faith in God would get me to heaven someday, but it had very little relevance to the rest of my life. What most mattered to me was being accepted by my peer group.

Transferring to public high school from a Christian school our freshman year had made my classmates and I "outsiders" and the subject of ridicule. The public school kids were mean to us and called us "fags" just because we were Christians. I did not appreciate being stereotyped, so I began to distance myself from former Christian school classmates, which put me in a no-man's-land within the cliquish high school landscape. I desperately wanted acceptance into the "in crowd." I was in a state of social purgatory until my junior year when I began to excel in sports and thus earned access to all the cool parties. I saw it as a rite of passage and drank more and acted crazier than anyone. Pretty soon I was known as Party Marty. Kids would typically gather in The Grove, a stand of walnut trees by the river, yet the party did not officially start until Mike and I pulled up in my shiny Toyota with cases of beer and the stereo booming rock and roll.

One Sunday morning after a night of partying, I was awakened by my mother's pleading voice calling downstairs to my room. "Marty, get up! It's time to go to church." I managed to drag myself out of bed, because going to church was not optional in the Meyer house. I looked in the mirror through bloodshot eyes with a splitting headache, and I actually hated what I saw. I began to speak with self-loathing. "Marty, you are such a hypocrite. You're going to go to church to confess your sins, but will go out next week and do the exact same things. You're such a big fake." It was far from a prayer, but I believe the Father took it as my plea for rescue in leaving a life of self-destruction.

Within a week my dad announced to our family that he had accepted a new position as a nursing home director. We would be moving to the small town of Minneapolis in north-central Kansas. Dad would relocate immediately; the rest of the family would join him after the school year ended. I was shocked by his decision. Didn't he realize next year was my senior year? That I was poised to be a starter for a football team expected to rise to the state championship? I was so angry that it fueled and justified my downward spiraling behavior.

Mike's younger brother Matt and I had already "done church" that partly cloudy spring day, so we resolved to indulge in a lazy afternoon.

The road to Tunnel Mill Dam transitions to gravel before bending up the dike and over railroad tracks. It then arcs through a park of massive walnut trees before reaching the river. With music blasting, we flew up the embankment toward an uncontrolled railroad crossing. Suddenly the raucous rock and roll was muted by the deafening brass of a locomotive's warning horn. We had not seen or heard the train, but now the thundering beast bore down on us at top speed, in full view. I desperately jammed the brakes. My wheels struggled to grip wet gravel as we slid onto the vibrating tracks. In strange slow motion the locomotive's massive grill crushed into the passenger side door where Matt sat. I felt the car rise from the tracks, and thrown like a rag doll, roll violently down the embankment. Neither of us wore seatbelts, and we tumbled inside the car like shoes in a dryer. At one point I realized that Matt was circling up toward the roof as the car careened down for another roll. Somehow I managed to reach up and fling him into the back seat just as the top of the car slammed onto the ground below. My golden Corolla came to an abrupt stop, right side up, as it met hard with a telephone pole.

Miraculously, Matt and I escaped without a scratch. With violent pounding in our chests, we crawled out a mangled opening, which had formerly been the rear window. The twisted remains of my beloved car lay in a pool of shattered glass. As the train grinded to a halt, Matt and I made our way mindlessly back up to the road. I do not recall how long we stood there, dazed, over the wreckage, but I do remember my lone, pathetic declaration: "Oh my God, my car is ruined!" The lights and siren of an ambulance screamed toward us and jarred us back into clearer consciousness. However, completely ignoring Matt and me, three paramedics jumped out of their vehicle and frantically began searching the wreckage. Finally, bewildered, one of the paramedics approached us and asked, "Where are the bodies?"

"I'm not sure what you mean," I stammered.

"The people who were in that car," he insisted. "Where are the bodies?"

I was both horrified and relieved by the reality of this question. "We are the bodies," I softly responded. "I was the driver of that vehicle." By this time the train engineer approached, awkwardly running along the railroad ties with a burning question most certainly racing through his mind: Did the two young men in that car make it out alive? He was just as relieved and perplexed as the paramedics to discover that Matt and I were the unscathed boys from the twisted carnage. "How could that be? There's not a cut or bruise on either one of you," the engineer said.

I could not comprehend it at the time, but looking back, I'm fully aware that the hand of God spared our lives that Sunday afternoon. His guardian angels covered us and protected us. I had no idea then that God had a plan for my life and would not allow it to prematurely end that day on the way to Tunnel Mill Dam. Instead, all I could think about was my car and how I would have to call my dad and tell him what I had done.

Not only did God spare me from death that day, but he was graciously crushing a "golden idol" in my life. An idol is anything that captures our heart and steals our affections, which rightfully belong to our Creator and Savior. The Father desires to have a relationship with us, his children, but we displace him with all manner of things. Important to me were my friends, my car, and how that glittery idol served my pursuit of acceptance.

The kids at school were ruthless when they found out what happened. They would come up behind me and make loud horn noises, calling me "train man" and mockingly ask where my slick car was now. Overnight, I seemed to have destroyed whatever popularity and acceptance I had managed to gain. I tried to laugh it off and play it cool, but at night, the distant sound of a screeching train would pull me back into that nightmarish moment of staring into a barreling mass of steel seconds before impact. I would awake in a cold sweat and struggle to return to sleep, wondering why I was still alive.

Though I didn't know it at the time, God heard my heart cry and in response began removing idols from my life. Idols have a fatal way of taking our eyes off God, where our true faith is found. Epic faith requires a refining process that redirects our focus solely back to him. Simply having knowledge of God's Word is not enough. God was preparing my heart to encounter the Author of Life. I would soon discover a radical relationship with the Word.

TWO

My Best Friend

MINNEAPOLIS, Kansas, ended up being everything I feared. The tiny rural town seemed like a road to nowhere. Its sole claim to fame was Rock City, a national landmark on the outskirts of town, a bizarre garden of spherical rock formations strewn about on a patch of prairie as if placed there by a gigantic ice cream scoop. My senior class had about thirty students, and I did not care to befriend any of them. I regarded my life as an ordeal. I figured that I would only be here for one year and then head back to Winfield to attend Saint John's College with my buddy Mike, where my dad had once worked as a professor.

While my former football team in Winfield amassed wins and advanced toward a state championship, my new Minneapolis team lost every single game. I recalled how Coach Markley back in Winfield had invited me to stay: "Rookie, why do you want to go to Minneapolis, Kansas? You should stay here and play for me. You'll be one of my starting tight ends." Sadly, staying was never an option, and thinking about where I could have been felt like salt in an open wound. I was stuck in a loser town with a losing football team whose quarterback could not even throw a football.

After my train encounter in Winfield, popularity had disillusioned me. It hurt when those whom I considered friends had targeted me for ridicule. Real friendship was not in reach, so I became guarded, telling myself that I didn't care. Yet deep inside I longed for true companionship. I wanted to embrace someone trustworthy. Was there anyone who could understand me, a confidant with whom to share my inner thoughts, emotions, and the questions racing through me?

One evening I retreated to my bedroom early. In a moment of loneliness and longing, the words of a childhood Sunday school teacher drifted across my mind: *Jesus is your best friend.*

I nearly laughed out loud. "Some kind of friend you've been, Jesus," I muttered to myself. "I can't see you or talk to you. I don't need some kind of imaginary friend right now. I need someone who's real. Someone who can understand what I'm going through."

More words from my Sunday school teacher flooded my mind: *Jesus is a friend who loves you no matter what happens in life. You can get to know him by reading the Bible.*

"Fine. You want to be my friend, Jesus?" In a cocky rebuttal I resolved to confront the thoughts head-on. But in the midst of resistance my heart betrayed me, and my complaint melted into a desperate plea. "Jesus, if you are really real, then I want to know you. I want you to be my best friend, and I want to be yours. I've believed in you, but now I need you to make yourself real to me."

During this spontaneous prayer, I had discovered my Bible under a blanket of dust. It had been presented to me four years earlier on completion of my church's confirmation class, and I now clutched it urgently as I continued my supplication. "Jesus, I ask that you would make yourself real to me through this book. Would you come alive in my heart as I read about you?"

I knew where to find the stories about Jesus, so I turned to the Gospel of Matthew. My Bible creaked with stiffness as I opened it.

I broke that Bible in for hours that night, reading with intrigue about a God who came to the earth as a helpless baby. I was fascinated by Jesus the boy—that he did not fit in, and how he was drawn to the temple to encounter the Scriptures. I pictured Jesus approaching the muddy banks of the Jordan River, where he was baptized by his cousin John. I imagined him at the sea of Galilee calling the first disciples, asking them to drop their fishing nets to follow him, and there, summoning me as well.

Turning page after page in my Bible, I finally clicked off the bedside light. My mind reeled with stories I had just read and people I had just encountered for the first time. I drifted off to sleep that night with an uncharacteristic peace, transformation beginning deep within my heart.

The next day unfolded as usual with school, football practice, and dinner with my parents and younger sister Carrie, my only sibling still at home. I found myself antsy to get back to my room. Without even watching my regular TV programs, I announced that I would be going to bed early. Then, in the seclusion of my bedroom, I again held my Bible and prayed a simple prayer. "Jesus, I ask that you would show yourself to me. I want to know you as my best friend. I pray that you would bring this book to life." Just like the night before, with each turn of the page I discovered something new about a remarkable friend named Jesus.

For the next several months this became my daily pattern. Each night I retreated to my room, clutched my Bible, and asked Jesus to reveal himself to me. Something indescribable took place. Jesus, the Son of God, walked out of the pages of the Bible and became as real to me as any person I knew in this world.

Just before Easter I read the crucifixion account in the book of Luke, a story I had heard hundreds of times. This time, tears streamed down my face. I read how the soldiers mocked Jesus, spit on him, and whipped him until the flesh on his back was raw. I wept because I realized for the first time that they did this to my best friend.

When they placed his arm against the cross's rough wood and drove spikes through the flesh and bone of his hands and feet, I realized that my friend Jesus was willingly doing this for me. He had done nothing wrong. My sins demanded his sacrifice. I recalled a verse that I had found in the book of Isaiah:

Surely he took up our infirmities and carried our sorrows, yet we
considered him stricken by God, smitten by him, and afflicted.
But he was pierced for our transgressions, he was crushed for
our iniquities; the punishment that brought us peace was upon
him, and by his wounds we are healed. (Isa. 53:4–5)

I began to think of all the stupid and selfish things I had done,
about how rebellious I had been and my disrespectful attitude toward
my parents and others. The realization hit me: it cost Jesus everything
to pay for my senseless sin. I began to cry out, "Oh Jesus, I am so sorry.
My sin nailed you to that cross. You did this so that I could be forgiven.
You are the best friend anyone could ever hope for. Jesus, you took my
place. I deserve this punishment, but you went to the cross for me."

I recalled the words of Jesus I had read in John 15:13: "Greater love
has no one than this, that he lay down his life for his friends." That's
what he did for me. Jesus did not reject me—he forgave me. I felt the
weighty burden of my sin lift off my shoulders as I acknowledged the
forgiveness for which Jesus paid with his life. I felt free, the shame of my
past behind me.

A sinking awareness came—that it was I who had been the unfaith-
ful friend. The realization hit me like a linebacker. I had resented being
betrayed by friends and had even accused Jesus of not being there for
me. I had known of God's love and forgiveness since I was a child but
had treated these gifts with contempt. "Jesus, after all you have done for
me, I have to admit what a terrible friend I have been." My confession
was painful and liberating at the same time. "I've finally grasped that
you are my best friend. Now I want to be your friend."

At this point I had been poring over the Scriptures each evening for
months and found that only Abraham, Moses, and Job had been desig-
nated as "God's friend." Yet Jesus seemed to open up this opportunity
to all:

You are my friends if you do what I command. I no longer call you
servants, because a servant does not know his master's business.
Instead, I have called you friends, for everything that I learned
from my Father I have made known to you." (John 15:14–15)

Through the Word of God, my loneliness and longing was replaced by faith and friendship with Jesus. Epic faith is built upon God's Word because through it, we come to know God. Faith grows as we develop a living relationship with our Savior.

My transformation was far from complete. I would soon discover that Jesus was not only my friend and Savior. He also wanted to be the Lord of my life.

THREE

The Lord of My Life

AFTER graduating from high school in Minneapolis, Kansas, I met up with my brother Rob to work at Camp Perkins, a church camp in the heart of central Idaho's Sawtooth Mountains. This was becoming our summer tradition. My brother and I were close even though he was nine years older. He was a teacher at a Christian school, freeing his summers to spend in Idaho.

One day while reading my Bible I came across some verses about fasting. I didn't know what that was, so I asked Rob.

"Fasting is when you go without food in order to focus on God," he explained.

"Have you ever done it?" I asked. Rob replied that he had fasted on several occasions and that it helped him grow in his faith. That was all I needed to hear. "Then I won't be at lunch today," I stated matter-of-factly.

I didn't know exactly what to do, so I took my Bible and went down to the lake, where I found a nice rock to sit on. For the longest time I just stared across at the beautiful mountains while the constant sound of the waves gently lapped against the rocks at my feet. God was inviting me to know him more deeply. I read some of my favorite Bible verses and spent some time talking with Jesus. It was nothing spectacular, but I certainly felt closer to God. I went back to work on our afternoon projects, and by the time dinner rolled around, I was famished.

I was scheduled to begin at Saint John's College in a liberal arts program that fall, so after the summer I headed back to Kansas. Saint John's didn't have a football team, so when I arrived I tried out for varsity soccer as a walk-on. I had never played soccer competitively, so I figured I would try being a goalkeeper. As a tight end in football I had "good hands" and reaction time. I lived by Coach Markley's creed: "Rookie, if you can touch it, you can catch it." I made it onto the team, and less than halfway through the season was promoted to starting goalie. I would later be ranked third nationally in the NCAA Division 3 as a goalkeeper and receive the athlete of the year award.

My achievements started going to my head. I always had a strong will and found that I could succeed in nearly anything I set my mind to. By the time I returned to Camp Perkins the following summer, my feelings of invincibility were firmly established. I felt in control of my life, its possibilities endless. As an added ego boost, this was the summer I would be promoted to the counselor team. I arrived early to help develop the program for the campers.

One day after lunch I asked Mark, the program director, if I could borrow his motorcycle, a hefty 650cc Yamaha road bike. I assured him that I knew how to ride. After all, I was practically an expert, having ridden a total of three times before. Mark said okay. I didn't even bother grabbing a helmet; in an instant I was gone.

How exhilarating to fly up the high mountain pass of Galena Summit with the wind in my hair. I was whipping left and leaning right as I sped around each bend. I didn't say it aloud, but my inflated emotions proclaimed "I'm in control of my life and can achieve anything I set my heart on doing." I headed back, but when I reached the turnoff to the camp, I decided that my fun wasn't finished. Rather than hitting the brakes, I gave it more gas, speeding past the camp on a road alongside the lake. *Let's see what this baby can do*, I thought as I twisted the throttle wide open on a straightaway. I looked down to see the speedometer boasting 80 mph and climbing. I don't know how much speed I carried into the next curve, but I discovered quickly its danger. Without warning I found myself in the gravel on the extreme right edge of road. It was too late to brake, and leaning the bike more would grab no pavement.

In that moment absolute certainty flooded me: I was going to die. An odd peace came over me in what I perceived to be my final seconds of life. Without fear, I breathed, "Jesus, take me home."

When I opened my eyes, the deepest brilliant color of blue flooded me. *Heaven is blue,* I thought. *How wonderful. That's my favorite color.* I glanced to my left and noticed a stand of rich green pine trees, marveling that they grew in heaven as I had always hoped. My head shifted slightly to the right, the image of a mangled motorcycle jarring me back into reality. My thoughts were racing. *I've been in a terrible accident. Can I even move?* In a daze, I willed myself to my feet and somehow stood beside the road. I placed my left hand on the back of my head, bewildered by its softness, much like an over-ripe tomato. I pulled my hand away and watched it drip with blood. Even in shock, I realized I needed aid. I lay down by the side of the road and prayed, "Jesus, please send someone to help me. I need you now more than ever."

The next thing I remember was the sound of a vehicle approaching. I struggled to my feet and began to wave with my left hand, forgetting that it was soaked with blood. A US Forest Service truck stopped, and I instinctively crawled into the cab. "Take me to Camp Perkins," I managed.

Perhaps because my return had been overdue, my brother Rob met the service truck promptly at the camp entrance. Moments later we were speeding in Rob's car to the clinic in Stanley, Idaho. Upon arrival, medics strapped me to a gurney and transferred me by ambulance over the mountain summit to the hospital in Ketchum. The paramedics wheeled me in for X-rays and the doctors discovered that I had two compressed lower vertebrae, but beyond that nothing that time and rest would not heal. A doctor stitched up a huge gash on the back of my head, and nurses took me to my room to be observed through the night.

Once settled in my hospital room, my brother let me know that he would return in the morning to check up on me. Though dreading his departure, I wore a brave face. After Rob left, Loneliness and Rejection visited me. I fought to keep these old friends at bay and wondered why my true friend, Jesus, seemed so distant. Had he forsaken me when I needed him most?

In physical and emotional pain, I reached for the bedside drawer. It glided open and revealed what I had hoped: a Gideon Bible. I brought out the crisp, embossed hardcover and clenched it between my hands. "Jesus, I want you to speak to me through your Word," I managed to whisper. "I guess I've been trying to do things on my own. I'm sorry. Would you speak to me now?" Although not my normal practice, I determined to open the book with my eyes closed and consider the page I beheld as God's word to me.

Looking back on this scene, I imagine an unseen angelic being, with one stroke of its wing, causing the Bible to part to Jesus' intended page. When I opened my eyes, these illuminated words leaped off the page:

Young men, in the same way be submissive to those who are older. All of you, clothe yourselves with humility toward one another, because, "God opposes the proud but gives grace to the humble." Humble yourselves, therefore, under God's mighty hand, that he may lift you up in due time. Cast all your anxiety on him because he cares for you. (1 Pet. 5:5–7)

The passage hit me intensely, harder than the bloody wreck I had just survived. I had thought that I was in control of my life. Pride had blinded me to the reality that I had betrayed my best friend. I had not realized that friendship with Jesus, unlike human friendship, requires obedience.

"Oh God, I thought that I was in control of my life," I began, "but now I realize that my life is in your hands. If I'm the one that's driving, I'm certainly going to wreck everything. Today, Jesus, I give you control of my life. You are not just my Savior—you are the Lord of my life. I want you to take over. I give myself to you."

Had I died that day alongside that mountain highway, there is no doubt in my mind that I would have gone to heaven to be with Jesus. Still, it was becoming clear to me that God had a purpose for my life. I had been so absorbed with Jesus' friendship yet had somehow missed other important aspects in my relationship with God. Now he was teaching me what it meant to follow Jesus, to submit to his will, and to sacrifice my desires for his glory.

I began the process of physical recovery, and by the time the first group of kids poured into camp two weeks later, I was ready for them. I found great fulfillment by investing in the lives of young people and teaching them how meaningful a relationship with Jesus Christ could be. As God taught me, I immediately instructed others. The camp, and my renewed direction, became a lush greenhouse for spiritual growth.

Like many of the heroes of faith I had read about in the Bible, I had to be broken before I could see that God's plans and purposes are better than my own. Epic faith learns to yield to God and to give him room to determine our future. I was about to experience another major course correction.

FOUR

A Passion for the Word

BY the time I returned for my second year of college at Saint John's, serious questions about my direction in life troubled me. Instead of liberal arts, I felt the Lord tugging on my heart, pointing me toward full-time ministry. (Had my former high school teachers heard that I was even considering this, they would have died a collective heart attack.) I found a Christian education program that interested me, one that would allow me to combine ministry with two of my other passions—exploring the outdoors and impacting young people. This, however, introduced a problem: it would require me to leave Saint John's.

By the time spring break rolled around, I knew I had to decide. I went home to visit my parents. "Home" was now Saint Louis, Missouri, where they had both grown up and were now taking care of my aging grandparents. I told my father that I wanted to take him out for breakfast. Looking over cups of coffee and Egg McMuffins, I caught his quizzical gaze. He finally broke the ice, "So, what did you want to talk to me about?"

I had a hard time getting started. I had changed so much in the last few years that even I had trouble coming to grips with it. I finally spilled out an ironic and almost comical statement: "I've been considering going into full-time ministry—" The admission did not humor or ruffle my father; his eyes pleaded for me to continue. "I'm thinking about transferring to the Saint Paul University Christian education program in Minnesota," I continued, my utterance as much a question as a statement. "Dad, I just don't know what to do. Tell me if you think I should become a minister."

"Son," he began, "of course I would be happy to see you go into ministry, but I would be just as proud of you if you choose a different path. This is a choice for you to make. You can't make this decision to please me and I can't make it for you. I am very proud of you and know that you will make the right choice."

I struggled to restrain the tears streaming down my face. In a culture with very few rites of passage, my dad had just pronounced me a man.

After this experience, I gained confidence to make the decision I knew Jesus had drawn my heart toward. Upon my return from spring break I informed my closest friends, Mike and Doyle, that I would transfer from Saint John's to Saint Paul's University the following year. Their disappointment was evident, but I felt clearly the approval of my best friend, Jesus.

Once settled in Saint Paul, I excelled in my studies, especially Bible classes. I had struggled academically since grade school. In fact, a high school guidance counselor had told me outright that my abilities were insufficient for success in college, and that I should consider vocational training instead. Yet by my second semester at Saint Paul, I dove into twenty-one credit hours and pulled a 4.0, which did wonders for my GPA.

One day during an Old Testament class, the professor asked a question no one seemed willing to answer, so I tentatively raised my hand. My response so astounded the teacher that he asked where I had learned that. I explained, "I've been reading my Bible every day for the past few years. Before I start, I ask Jesus to reveal himself to me so that I can know him better. Everything I know about the Bible, I learned from Jesus." He seemed skeptical at my response.

I soon realized that my approach, the one that came so natural for me, was too simplistic for biblical academics. To remedy this, I began learning how to debate doctrinal matters and back up my answers using the Bible. I excelled in theological studies and enjoyed outperforming my classmates in an academic approach to the Bible.

The following year I was assigned an internship at Messiah Church in Longmont, Colorado, with opportunity to test my wings overseeing a church's youth ministry and Bible education programs. The senior pastor assigned me the responsibility to read aloud the gospel (a selection from Matthew, Mark, Luke, or John) each Sunday. In this church it was a real honor to stand behind the altar and proclaim the selected Gospel reading. When finished, I would assert, "This is the Word of the Lord," and everyone in the congregation would respond with a hearty "Thanks be to God."

I wanted to perform readings competently and avoid the embarrassment of stumbling over difficult words or names. The gigantic altar Bible was a different translation from the one with which I was familiar, so I made it my habit to take it home each Friday to practice readings over the weekend. One Saturday night, panic flooded me when I realized I had forgotten to pick it up. I scurried to the church to recover the weighty book.

Unlocking the church door, I slipped along the wooden pews without bothering to switch on the lights. The spacious sanctuary had a grand vaulted ceiling that arched heavenward. Plush carpet silenced my footfalls as I approached the ornate altar. The ominous beauty of moonlight shone through stained glass windows.

Taking hold of the massive manuscript on the altar, I turned to leave but could not, something in my heart pleading to linger for a while. I sat quietly on the altar steps, pondering the treasure in my arms.

"Lord, I've dedicated my life to you and have a passion to know your Word," I prayed softly. I continued by reciting one of my favorite verses from Psalm 119: "Oh, how I love your law! I meditate on it all day long. Your commands make me wiser than my enemies, for they are ever with me. I have more insight than all my teachers, for I meditate on your statutes. I have more understanding than the elders, for I obey your precepts."

I considered my own journey involving the Scriptures. "This is where it all started. Lord, I remember the first time I clutched that old confirmation Bible and asked you to be my friend. Not much has changed since then. I'm still reading the Bible every day."

What I heard next from deep within pierced my heart with deadly accuracy.

"But back then, you read it just to know me."

Instantly I recognized God's firm yet loving rebuke—even a hint of sadness or longing in his voice. Did Jesus somehow miss me? Cut to the core, I realized I had subtly substituted knowing the Bible for knowing him. The memory of my own prayer back in high school echoed in my mind, convicting me: "Jesus, I want to be your friend, but I need you to make yourself real to me. As I read this book, I just want to know you."

By this time I was facedown on the floor. I poured my heart out to Jesus. "I'm so sorry that I've replaced you. I've made an idol out of knowing the Bible but have left you behind, shadowed by my ambition to 'serve' God. How could I have been such a fool? Jesus, bring me back to you, my friend and first love."

In my zeal to please my Bible professors, I had traded friendship with Jesus for the knowledge of the Scriptures. I wanted to recapture my simple approach of reading the Bible just to know God. I wanted Jesus to be my teacher and resolved to be his student and follow him with all my heart. In that quiet, ominous church, Jesus was reminding me that faith is rooted in my intimate friendship with him.

Epic faith learns to walk in intimacy with God. Knowing the Word is simply the pathway to knowing him. There was so much more that my friend Jesus wanted to teach me, but for me to grasp it, Jesus would need to introduce me to someone.

FIVE

There Must Be More

DESPITE my passion to know Jesus through his Word, I grappled with a lingering question about that late-night church experience. Was that really God speaking to me? I had not wanted to face the apparent contradiction between my church's doctrine and my own experience. My Bible teachers taught that God speaks to us through the Bible—the written Word—period. I interpreted this to mean that God said everything he ever wanted to say and wrote it down in a book, the Bible. Yet I also had my own experiences. In that quiet church, like so many other times in my journey of friendship with God, I had sensed his still small voice speaking deep within my heart. Or was that just me talking to myself? If so, why would it produce such profound conviction? Had I been limiting God by thinking that he would only speak through the Bible? I had an aching feeling there must be more.

Recalling a testimony from my older sister Julie, my internal struggle intensified. Several years previously Julie had begun attending a charismatic church. My dad was clearly not happy about that. I knew that our church denomination did not believe in that spirit-filled stuff, but I could not deny the vibrant change I saw in my sister. She seemed so sincere in her love and excitement about Jesus. Once I determined to confront her about it.

"Julie, you know our whole family is Christian," I began. "I just don't think it's something to get that excited about. I mean, you're starting to make some of us feel uncomfortable." My words sounded hollow and betrayed the longing in my own heart to experience the "something more" that I suspected she had actually found.

Julie explained that those in her church were receiving spiritual gifts, being baptized by the Holy Spirit, and being blessed with prayer language—all things I knew practically nothing about, even as a Bible student. She told me that most people received the gift of tongues by having the elders of the church lay hands on them and pray for them. But Julie had not allowed anyone to lay hands on her, telling me she wanted to receive the gift of tongues directly from Jesus. "One night I went to my dorm room at KU (University of Kansas) and decided I would pray until the Lord blessed me—all night if necessary," Julie said. "I began praying and asking God to fill me with his Spirit. As I prayed God began highlighting issues in my heart that he wanted to deal with. So I spent time repenting and receiving his forgiveness. The Holy Spirit lovingly yet firmly dealt with one issue after another. It was so cleansing. Then, I repeated my plea for Jesus to baptize me in his Spirit. I sat waiting and waiting, but nothing happened. Finally, I felt the gentle whisper of the Spirit telling me that I needed to open my mouth and let words come out. So I opened my mouth and began speaking. Out came a beautiful prayer language, in a tongue unknown to me. The joy I felt was beyond anything I had ever experienced before. I immediately knew that I had received the baptism of the Holy Spirit."

I was left wondering what all this meant for me. Though not sold on the idea of speaking in tongues, or even hearing God's voice, I desperately wanted to be close to him. Even though I knew little about the Holy Spirit and his gifts, I had a feeling my sister's testimony was a key to the "more" I was looking for. I began to pray for God to bless me with the Holy Spirit and any gifts I needed to know and serve him better.

I ventured out for long, late-night prayer walks around my college campus. "Jesus, would you introduce me to the Holy Spirit? I know he is part of the Trinity, but I don't know him. I want the work of the Spirit active in my life."

Because speaking in tongues seemed to ignite my sister Julie's passion for God, this was the gift I asked for. Yet no matter how hard I prayed or how much I believed, this gift eluded me. At times I complained to God, wondering why he did not grant my request. I did not realize he was not responding to what I wanted but instead giving me gifts I truly needed, just as I had asked.

While pleading with God for the gift of tongues, I had begun to pray the most beautiful prayers *from* him: "Marty, I love you. You are my son and I have great plans for you. I will always be with you and I will empower you for my purposes." I had never heard anyone pray like this, and failed to realize that the Holy Spirit was blessing me with a prophetic gift, one that the apostle Paul had regarded even greater than tongues for the building up of God's people. During my disappointment at prayers not answered as I expected, God was responding in my best interest, giving me what I actually requested. Though unperceived, the Holy Spirit was becoming a vibrant person in my life.

After completing my college education, I began serving diligently in my first official assignment, at Grace Church in Pocatello, Idaho. At Grace, as we called it, I was put in charge of junior and senior high youth ministries, Sunday school, adult Bible education, and volunteer coordination. With no shortage of work to be done, I was eager to jump right in. One of my favorite activities was teaching Bible study for youth on Monday nights. Instead of using an established curriculum, I'd have students choose a book from the Bible, and we would work through it together verse by verse, one chapter at a time. One of the ground rules was that they could ask any question they wanted. If I didn't know the answer, I would admit it honestly and ensure that I'd produce a response for them by the following week.

One week a bright and curious student named Amy came to class with a question. "I want to know about faith," she inquired.

I launched into a discourse about how one is saved by faith in Christ, but she cut me short. "I know all about that. I'm asking about the faith that, well, you do miracles and stuff with. It seems like people in the Bible did things by faith, and it makes me think that there's got to be more to faith than I've experienced." I felt my face flush as all the teenage eyes fixed on me. Amy had asked what everyone else was afraid to, and they keenly awaited my response. Secretly, I too was wrestling with the same question.

Dave, a fiery student, filled the awkward pause. "Yeah, Amy's right, we keep reading about the power of God in the Bible, but when's the last time we saw that power at work in real life? If the Bible is true, wouldn't we see the same things happening now?"

"I . . . I—" Stammering, I tried to answer Dave's questions off the cuff. I had been too embarrassed to admit that I knew little to satisfy their hunger to have this very basic question answered. Finally, I confessed that I needed more time to prepare an appropriate response.

My initial study raised more questions than answers, and I requested another week before offering my reply. The typically difficult verses did not trouble me so much. But I struggled with the "plain and simple" scriptures. I began a handwritten list of those verses on a yellow legal pad:

The prayer of a righteous man is powerful and effective. (James 5:16)

Now to him who is able to do immeasurably more than all we ask or imagine, according to his power that is at work within us. (Eph. 3:20)

Therefore I tell you, whatever you ask for in prayer, believe that you have received it, and it will be yours. (Mark 11:24)

I tell you the truth, anyone who has faith in me will do what I have been doing. He will do even greater things than these, because I am going to the Father. And I will do whatever you ask in my name, so that the Son may bring glory to the Father. You may ask me for anything in my name, and I will do it. (John 14:12–14)

Jesus could not possibly mean what I thought he meant, could he? The Bible seemed to be saying that there is a power, Jesus' resurrection power, within us, somehow accessed through faith. And with this power we can do even greater things than Jesus did while on the earth. While that would certainly answer Amy's question, the problem was that it didn't seem to work that way in my experience.

During the weeks I wrestled for an adequate response for Amy, I noticed that Dave had stopped attending our Monday night study. He had become such a spark plug in our group that he'd earned the nickname "Power Dave," and his absence was obvious. I asked around and learned that he had started a hard rock band. When I happened to see him one day and asked how he was doing, all Dave could talk about was his band. He even asked me to pray for the band: that they would "make it to the big time." I assured Dave that I would pray concerning his band.

That night I went before the Lord and prayed, "Lord Jesus, I am really concerned about my young friend Dave. This band he has started has become an idol in his life, leading him down the wrong path. I pray for his band to simply dissolve so that Dave's focus would return to you. In your name I pray. Amen."

The next Monday, Dave showed up at Bible study, the first time in quite a while. Before I could even ask, Dave launched into his complaint. "I thought you were going to pray for my band. I can't believe what happened. Last week everyone quit for no reason. How could God let this happen?" When I explained that I actually did pray for his band, confessing the nature of my prayer, he was understandably upset. "Dude! How could you pray against my band?" Dave protested. "That's just wrong."

Eventually, Dave got over being angry with me and later even thanked me. "I guess I knew deep in my heart that the band was leading me away from God," Dave admitted. "I just wanted it so bad that I ignored those feelings. Thanks for helping me get back on track."

Despite my experience in praying for Dave, I had yet to produce a satisfactory response for Amy and the rest of the gang. I petitioned the students for yet another week to prepare. I prayed that the Holy Spirit would lead me to the answers I was looking for. As I combed over the

Gospels again, something caught my eye: the way people approached Jesus when they had a need. I wondered, *Isn't that what we are doing when we pray? Approaching Jesus with our needs?*

My and my group's quest to see the power of God at work in our lives would require us to learn how to approach Jesus in faith.

SIX

Approaching Jesus in Faith

AFTER informing my students that we would finally grapple with Amy's question about faith, our Monday-night Bible study group packed into the basement of my small house. I began apprehensively, knowing that I did not yet possess the outright answers and walked only a small step ahead of the students in matters of putting faith into practice.

After our opening prayer, I drew in a deep breath and began, "First of all, we understand that saving faith is the starting point. We begin our faith walk by believing that Jesus died in sacrifice for our sins. We receive forgiveness, not because we do good works, but because we recognize that we are sinners in need of the Savior. We acknowledge what God did when he sent the Son, Jesus, by receiving his free gift of forgiveness and the promise of heaven." The students nodded patiently.

"I think this promise of eternal life begins right now," I continued. "We have missed the point if we think our faith is only to get us into heaven. Jesus died, and rose from the dead, so that we could have a relationship with him right now and live by the power of the Holy Spirit, who is alive in each of us who believes."

A quick survey of the room informed me that everyone was tracking, so I continued, "When we don't realize the 'something more' that we are looking for, it is because we have a passive approach. We simply sit back waiting for God to impress us, while Jesus desires for us to press into him with our faith. This week I've been studying the way people approached Jesus in the Bible, and I've found that it demanded much faith to bring their problems to him. What is more, they fully expected Jesus to do something about it. Let's open our Bibles to Matthew chapter eight."

The sound of fluttering pages saturated the place as eager teens found the first book of the New Testament. "You will notice at the end of chapter seven that everyone was amazed at Jesus' words because he taught with authority," I prefaced. "In chapter eight we will see that he demonstrates that authority. Now, who wants to start reading at verse one?"

Jim, a tall, lanky student, plodded through the first three verses:

When he came down from the mountainside, large crowds followed him. A man with leprosy came and knelt before him and said, "Lord, if you are willing, you can make me clean."

Jesus reached out his hand and touched the man. "I am willing," he said. "Be clean!" Immediately he was cured of his leprosy.

"Leprosy was a terribly contagious skin disease," I explained. "Once people got it, they had to go live in small communities with other lepers because no one was allowed to touch them. Now, what can we learn by the way the man with leprosy approached Jesus?"

"Well, it must have taken a lot of courage to leave the leper colony and go find Jesus," Amy suggested.

"And he must have been humble, because we see that he was kneeling before Jesus," Desiree chimed in.

Jim added, "I've never thought that Jesus is willing to help me with my problems. The man with leprosy questioned Jesus' willingness and found that Jesus was willing to touch him and heal him. If Jesus was willing to help the man with leprosy, then maybe he is willing to help me."

I noticed Jeff, a shy student, listening intently as Jim mused over Jesus' willingness to enter into our problems. Now we're getting somewhere, I thought. "Let's have someone continue reading verses five to thirteen."

Power Dave eagerly jumped in:

When Jesus had entered Capernaum, a centurion came to him, asking for help. "Lord," he said, "my servant lies at home paralyzed and in terrible suffering."

Jesus said to him, "I will go and heal him."

The centurion replied, "Lord, I do not deserve to have you come under my roof. But just say the word, and my servant will be healed. For I myself am a man under authority, with soldiers under me. I tell this one, 'Go,' and he goes; and that one, 'Come,' and he comes. I say to my servant, 'Do this,' and he does it."

When Jesus heard this, he was astonished and said to those following him, "I tell you the truth, I have not found anyone in Israel with such great faith. . . ."

Then Jesus said to the centurion, "Go! It will be done just as you believed it would." And his servant was healed at that very hour.

"What do you notice in this passage?" I asked.

"I've got this one," Dave continued. "The centurion was a powerful leader who understood authority. I think he recognized that Jesus had authority because he believed that Jesus was the Son of God. I love how the centurion says, 'Just say the word, Jesus, and I know it will be done!'"

"That's exactly right, Dave," I said, grateful for his presence in our group. "The centurion approached Jesus with faith that he had the authority to help him. Now I want you to notice something else. When Jesus healed the servant long-distance style, he said to the centurion, 'Go! It will be done just as you believed it would.' What does that say to us about the way we approach Jesus?"

Dave was on a roll. "It means that our own faith makes a huge difference. This military leader actually believed that Jesus would do it. That's a whole lot different than the way I usually pray. I sort of hope that Jesus will answer my prayers, but I'm not sure that he will. I guess we need to approach Jesus with confident belief that he has the ultimate authority and is willing to use it."

"That's great. I bet we can all think of things we need Jesus to help us with," I said. "What are some of the concerns Jesus addressed in these next few verses?" I continued reading:

> When Jesus came into Peter's house, he saw Peter's mother-in-law lying in bed with a fever. He touched her hand and the fever left her, and she got up and began to wait on him.
>
> When evening came, many who were demon-possessed were brought to him, and he drove out the spirits with a word and healed all the sick. This was to fulfill what was spoken through the prophet Isaiah: "He took up our infirmities and carried our diseases."

"It looks like nothing is too difficult for Jesus," Eric suggested. "It says here that he healed every disease and drove out the evil spirits. That's kind of freaky."

"But it's also saying that nothing is too small for Jesus," Amy said. "Look, he touches Peter's mother-in-law and she only had a fever. I don't think I would even bother Jesus if I had something as small as a headache. I guess I need to learn to approach Jesus with everything."

Energy was building in the room as the youth contemplated what it would mean to approach Jesus with great faith, just like the individuals they were reading about. "Okay, I'd like to look at a few more stories in chapter nine. Let's skip ahead to verse eighteen; this is really two stories with the same lesson."

Desiree began reading with a clear and confident voice:

> While he was saying this, a ruler came and knelt before him and said, "My daughter has just died. But come and put your hand on her, and she will live." Jesus got up and went with him, and so did his disciples.

Just then a woman who had been subject to bleeding for twelve years came up behind him and touched the edge of his cloak. She said to herself, "If I only touch his cloak, I will be healed."

Jesus turned and saw her. "Take heart, daughter," he said, "your faith has healed you." And the woman was healed from that moment.

When Jesus entered the ruler's house and saw the flute players and the noisy crowd, he said, "Go away. The girl is not dead but asleep." But they laughed at him. After the crowd had been put outside, he went in and took the girl by the hand, and she got up. News of this spread through all that region.

"What is one thing you see in common in these two stories?" I asked.

Amber responded hesitantly, "They both wanted Jesus to touch them?"

"But Jesus didn't touch the woman—she touched him," Dave said.

"In those days, the woman's 'issue of blood' would have made her ceremonially 'unclean,'" I instructed. "No one would have been allowed to even touch her. That's why she must have reasoned that she would have to touch him. Okay, keep your bookmark here while we take a look at Luke's account of the same story. He adds some details that give us additional insight."

Everyone listened as Eric read Luke 8:42–48.

As Jesus was on his way, the crowds almost crushed him. And a woman was there who had been subject to bleeding for twelve years, but no one could heal her. She came up behind him and touched the edge of his cloak, and immediately her bleeding stopped.

"Who touched me?" Jesus asked.

When they all denied it, Peter said, "Master, the people are crowding and pressing against you."

But Jesus said, "Someone touched me; I know that power has gone out from me."

Then the woman, seeing that she could not go unnoticed, came trembling and fell at his feet. In the presence of all the people, she told why she had touched him and how she had been instantly healed. Then he said to her, "Daughter, your faith has healed you. Go in peace."

"Whoa. Jesus felt the power going out of him and knew that someone got healed just by touching him," Dave blurted. "Now how cool is that?"

"It's kind of funny how Jesus asked, 'Who touched me?' when everyone around was crushed together and touching him," Amy added. "Think how confused the disciples must have been."

"Do you want to know what I think?" I said. "Jesus was so impressed with this woman that he wanted to meet the person who received healing just by touching him in faith. Have any of us ever thought about our prayers as touching Jesus? Do you think your prayers are more like the people who were crowding around Jesus or more like the woman who touched him in faith?"

"Back to what I said before," Jim said, "I think my prayers have been more like the crowd than the woman. I'm not sure that I've really thought my prayers would make any difference."

"But her prayers did make the difference," Amy added. "Look what Jesus said to the woman when he finally found her: 'Take heart, daughter, your faith has healed you.' There it is again. Our faith makes a difference."

"Exactly," I encouraged. "I think it's a key understanding for us. Now, let's go back to the book of Matthew. After Jesus healed the woman with the bleeding issue he continued following the man whose daughter had just died. In verse 23 we see that people had already begun to mourn the girl's death. They all laughed at the thought that Jesus could do anything about it. But the father wasn't laughing. I want you to think about how much faith it took for this man to go and get Jesus in the first place. Remember, this was the man who said, 'My daughter has just died. But come and put your hand on her, and she will live.' This man obviously had faith that Jesus had power even over death. Jesus simply took the girl by the hand and raised her to life. Do you see the power of his touch? I think we too can access that power by approaching Jesus with expectant faith."

"Now, there's one more story I wanted to cover tonight," I continued. "Who would like to continue reading Matthew 9:27–30?" Desiree took the initiative.

> As Jesus went on from there, two blind men followed him, calling out, "Have mercy on us, Son of David!"
>
> When he had gone indoors, the blind men came to him, and he asked them, "Do you believe that I am able to do this?"
>
> "Yes, Lord," they replied.
>
> Then he touched their eyes and said, "According to your faith will it be done to you"; and their sight was restored.

"What can we learn from this story?" I inquired.

"Look how bold these blind guys were to follow him and cry out for healing from Jesus," Dave said. "I'd call that approaching Jesus in faith."

"I noticed Jesus asked the blind men if they believed he was able to help," Desiree remarked. "I guess I sometimes question Jesus' ability to help me with the problems I'm facing."

"I get it," Eric added. "The blind men believed that Jesus was able to help them just like the centurion understood that Jesus had the authority to do it."

"And there's the thing about faith again," Amy added. "Jesus said, 'According to your faith will it be done to you.' The blind men received their sight because they approached Jesus with faith. That means that we can approach Jesus in faith and see him do miracles in our lives."

Amber shifted in her seat, a bit agitated by the direction our discussion was going. "Marty, do you really think our faith makes a difference? I've always gotten the impression that God is in charge and he is going to do whatever he is going to do, whether we pray about it or not—and whether we have faith or not. Which one is it: is God in control, or does he actually leave things up to us?"

"That's a great question," I responded. "Great minds have debated this issue for centuries. I'm beginning to wonder whether the answer might instead be a both/and for our limitless God."

"I don't understand," Amber pressed.

"We know from the Bible that God is sovereign—he is supreme and ultimately in control of all things," I said. "I'm not going to argue with that; it's a clear Bible truth. But we also learn that he asks us to pray in faith, and based on the scriptures we have just been studying, our faith makes a difference. These two truths seem to contradict each other. If God is really sovereign, how could my little prayers possibly make a difference? And how can God be in control if he leaves certain things up to us to carry out by faith? From our limited perspective, these ideas seem to be in conflict with each other.

"But let me throw another big word at you. It's the inscrutability of God. It means that there is a mysterious side of God beyond our comprehension. Look at what God says about himself in Isaiah 55:8–9, "'For my thoughts are not your thoughts, neither are your ways my ways,' declares the LORD. "As the heavens are higher than the earth, so are my ways higher than your ways and my thoughts than your thoughts.'" There are lots of things we can know about God, and many other things that we cannot even begin to understand. When we come to an area in the Bible that seems like a paradox, it may be because it falls into this area of the incomprehensible nature of God. There may be some things we humans are not meant to understand so that it leaves room for faith."

"I think you may have lost some of us there," Jim said.

"Okay, let's try a different approach. I found this scripture in my studies about faith. It's from the last part of Matthew chapter thirteen," I said to the accompaniment of fluttering pages of Bibles. "This section, beginning with verse 53, is talking about when Jesus went to Nazareth, his own hometown. People were amazed at his teaching, but they doubted his authority. They knew Jesus and his parents, his brothers and sisters, and they just thought of him as the little boy Jesus who grew up with their own children. How could he be someone special? Then the section ends with this verse, 'And he did not do many miracles there because of their lack of faith.' In Mark's account of the same story, in chapter six, he writes, 'He could not do any miracles there, except lay his hands on a few sick people and heal them. And he was amazed at their lack of faith.'

"We've been looking at all these people who received miracles because they approached Jesus in faith. In contrast, here are people who limited Jesus because of their lack of faith. We might think, 'How could we possibly limit God?' What if God prefers to work through us and our faith is actually a factor by which he has chosen to limit himself?"

I continued, "I've personally started praying this prayer: 'Lord, I don't want to limit you because of my unbelief. I want to pray with all my heart and leave the results up to you.' I don't understand why God seems to answer some of my prayers and not others. But what if each of us could start a faith experiment and approach Jesus as if it all depended on us, and then simply trust God for all the results."

The students began to reel with excitement as they realized that they could approach Jesus wholeheartedly and expect results. They had just been given permission to exercise their faith.

"Let's do it," Amy said, rallying. "Let's do the experiment. Let's all make a list of ten things we want to approach Jesus in faith about, and let's ask him to do miracles in our lives."

"That's an excellent suggestion," I said. "Let's all start a personal top-ten list of things we want to see God do in our lives. And let's not forget to put at the top of that list some of the people we want to come to Jesus as their Savior. Come ready to share your list next Monday when we continue our discussion."

I was so excited to see the students' enthusiasm. They were learning to trust the Bible and use it as their foundation to pray with expectant faith. However, my growing optimism would soon be confronted. How could I have possibly been prepared for the premature testing of my own ability to approach Jesus in faith?

SEVEN

Tested Faith

THE clock read 6:04 a.m. when my ringing phone forced me out of bed. *Who could be calling this early on a Saturday morning?* I answered the phone and was greeted by the familiar voice of Donna, our church secretary, but her tone was grave. My body froze as she relayed the news: "Jeff has committed suicide. Pastor wanted you to know and thought you would want to be with his parents. They are at the hospital now."

I managed to say, "I'll be there in fifteen minutes," but when I hung up the phone, I could hardly move. How could this be possible? My mind began to reel. My thoughts traveled immediately to the previous Wednesday, when I had taken Jeff four-wheeling in my off-road pickup. His parents and others were concerned about him, so I'd decided to spend some time with him. I'd picked Jeff up from his high school, and we headed straight for the hills. I could still hear his laughter as we bumped up steep foothills surrounding Pocatello, a laugh I'm not sure I'd ever heard before.

My truck roared toward the hospital while my mind mulled over the past few weeks. Each Monday night our youth group had been building our study about approaching Jesus with faith. There had been a buzz of excitement as students began to share praise reports from their top-ten prayer lists. Some reported healing, others said that Jesus was restoring family relationships, and several shared the exciting news of leading friends to faith in Christ. But Jeff had been more quiet than usual, hardly saying a word as we reviewed scriptures. As I drove to the hospital, I recited one of those verses from memory:

> I tell you the truth, anyone who has faith in me will do what I have been doing. He will do even greater things than these, because I am going to the Father. And I will do whatever you ask in my name, so that the Son may bring glory to the Father. You may ask me for anything in my name, and I will do it. (John 14:12–14)

Hot tears stung my eyes as I cried out from the cab of my truck, "Oh God, what good is faith now that Jeff is dead?"

Jeff's parents stood in the ER waiting room. "What happened?" I asked as I embraced them.

"It looks like it was an overdose," Jeff's dad pronounced as Jeff's mom wept softly. "We found him too late. There was nothing we could do." He looked at me through tear-filled eyes. "Marty, do you want to see him?"

It came as a request more than a question, so I complied. My feet, however, hesitated, and resisted the line to the adjacent room, feeling unprepared for what I would observe. Jeff's mom gently slid the sheet down below his face to reveal his thin, pale features. Numbness overcame my whole body at Jeff's now expressionless state.

A doctor entered the room to address Jeff's parents. "I need to discuss some things with you," he said. They followed him out the door.

I wanted to leave also, but my legs were frozen. The door swung closed behind them, leaving me with alone with Jeff. Inexplicably, I reached out and touched his hand but immediately withdrew it at the icy contact. I forced a desperate prayer, "Oh, Jesus, come near to us now."

"Pray that he may be raised to life," came Jesus' bold reply. But rather than responding in faith, I froze like the lifeless body I had just recoiled from.

The dark grip of death choked the air, suffocating and frightening me. I forced myself to recite Jesus' words, "I am the resurrection and the life." I tried to muster the faith to respond, "Jesus, I know you healed the sick and raised the dead, but you are God. How could you ask me to pray for Jeff, now? It's too late, Lord. I'm just a man." The weight of the moment stifled the faith that I had been proclaiming. I knew the Word of God: not only Jesus but also Peter, Elijah, and Elisha were credited with raising the dead. But how could I possibly rise to that level of faith?

I labored to dismiss the notion that Jesus had just spoken to me. I foolishly rationalized—what good would it do to see Jeff raised from the dead with his brain already damaged by the overdose? I failed to grasp that One who has power to raise the dead can surely heal a damaged brain. In my heart I felt like a failure. Riddled with self-doubt, I attempted to pray, "Lord, you can do all things. If you wanted to, you could even bring Jeff back to life." Yet my words sounded hollow and contrived. To my relief, a nurse interrupted, finding me alone with the deceased, and indicated it best if I return to the waiting room.

I left confused, ashamed, and determined to forget about what had happened in that room alone with Jeff's body, resolving never to speak about it. The event haunted me with unanswered questions. Was that really Jesus prompting me to pray? What if I had mustered the faith required to raise Jeff from the dead? Was the Lord just testing my obedience, or would I have seen God do a profound miracle? What good is believing the Bible if I lack the faith to actually practice it? In the days that followed, I wrestled with those questions and was forced to reevaluate what it meant to apply the Bible in taking steps of faith and obedience.

I was asked to speak at the funeral, and Manfred, our pastor at Grace Church, would officiate. I would have to address a question that kept surfacing: "Would Jeff go to heaven even if he committed suicide?" I knew Jeff had believed in Jesus, and I had talked with him about his faith just days before on that sunny afternoon ride in my pickup. I was unwilling to conclude, as some do, that Jeff had committed an unpardonable sin, but reasoned from Scripture that Jesus' forgiveness covers all sins, even the taking of one's own life. I knew Jeff was a confused young man who struggled with depression. But I also knew that he expressed faith in Christ, and in this I took comfort and hope.

The following Monday night we were scheduled to meet at my house for our weekly Bible study. Students began to show up early, wanting to talk about Jeff's death and the reality of having faith in Christ. By the time we were ready to start, there were too many kids to pack into my basement. We had to hold the meeting upstairs, and those that could not fit inside the house occupied the front and back porches, listening from outside. We had over 125 students, many of whom I had never met, asking difficult questions and eager to hear how having faith in Christ could make a difference in their lives. What impressed me most was how the core of twenty-five regular attenders honestly admitted that they did not understand everything, yet they defended their faith and testified how Jesus was making a difference in their own lives. They applied the very faith principles that we had been learning, inspiring others to take the first step of faith by believing in Christ. As a result, we saw many students come to a saving faith in Jesus.

In this season, weekly miracles resulted from our top-ten prayer experiment. I began each Monday night with an invitation, "Who has a praise report? What did you see God do this week? Did you have a miracle from your top-ten prayer list?" This became the weekly highlight as students gave glory to God for both big and small miracles they were seeing. And sometimes they brought miracles along.

"This is my friend Shellie," Amy announced one Monday. "Last week I told her about my faith in Jesus, and she wanted to come to our Bible study to learn more about him."

One night, Power Dave presented us with a special challenge. "I've been thinking about Saul, the guy in the Bible who used to kill Christians. He was the last person anyone would think would become a follower of Jesus. But you know the story—he met Jesus in a vision and became a Christian. In fact, he became the apostle Paul."

All eyes fixed on Dave while I wondered if he had a clear point or just planned to give a mini-sermon. I motioned with my hand for him to wrap it up.

"Well, I realized that if God can reach Saul, he can reach anyone. So, I'm thinking, why don't we start praying for the people we know who are the least likely to come to Jesus?"

The rest of the students jumped on it, and within minutes they had identified several "Sauls" from their high schools to put on their collective top-ten list. Sure enough, before the school year ended, at least one Saul had come to faith in Christ.

Our church endured the crisis of Jeff's death and, through it, discovered that we were being stretched in our faith. We honored Jeff by using his tragedy to tell others about our unshakeable faith in Jesus in the face of all our trials. I asked the Lord's forgiveness for my personal failure to summon faith when I needed it most, and committed myself to grow in my ability to put faith into practice.

Tragedy had tested me, just as it does for anyone walking out epic faith. The Bible explains that a refining process occurs when we endure pain, grief, or trial. It says, "These have come so that your faith—of greater worth than gold, which perishes even though refined by fire—may be proved genuine and may result in praise, glory and honor when Jesus Christ is revealed" (1 Pet. 1:7). Our faith is something so precious that it needs to be tested and refined to appropriate its value. Our own pain fires this furnace.

In this refining process, our church family was learning that if we really believe the Bible, we must live it. We would soon discover how doing the Word of God causes our faith to grow.

EIGHT

Putting It into Practice

M Y palms sweated and my heart raced—a natural reaction when speaking to over 250 people. Still, a convergence of events intensified this particular Sunday. Much had transpired since Jeff's death four years prior and my own resolution to practice the Word of God. Through preaching a message, I was recounting a journey our church family had been taking together.

The Bible talks about a personal and shared worship experience, yet our liturgy had remained so formal and rigid that it failed to connect to those unfamiliar with it. So my bride Kelly and I strove to start an engaging contemporary worship service. The elders eventually granted Kelly and me a Sunday morning time slot, thinking it no big deal if a few youth met in the sanctuary to sing camp songs. What soon developed differed much from their expectations. We created a community based on putting the Word into practice, one that reached all ages. Participants were so energized by the worship experience, which we called Living Praise, that they naturally invited their non-churched friends.

Within a year we had grown to a gathering of over a hundred, and within two years that number had doubled. Although our fresh, informal approach may have contributed to the draw, our focus remained: the practice of the Word of God—and this sustained our growth.

I looked over to Kelly, our gorgeous worship leader—my stunning wife. A contagious smile shone through her eyes as she led into the final song before my message. My thoughts drifted back six years to the first time the two of us had prayed together while working one summer at Camp Perkins.

We sat on the swimming docks, facing each other with eyes closed, as Kelly poured out her heart to God. Her prayer resounded so genuinely, her conversation with God so natural; I just had to peek. I parted my eyes and viewed Kelly praying wholeheartedly, then immediately heard a voice deep within my own heart: "This is the one."

I took that to be the Lord's affirmation that I would someday marry this girl who sang like an angel and prayed from her heart—but I never told her about the voice I heard on the dock until the day before our wedding. We started our relationship that summer, which turned into a long-distance relationship during that school year and those that followed, reuniting annually for our summers working together at camp.

I recalled my hurt and confusion when Kelly had broken up with me after four years of courtship just days before I left on a summer-long mission trip. I had no way of knowing that it was in part her own crisis of faith, not knowing if she was cut out to be "the minister's wife." Though my love for Kelly never fainted, I doubted I'd really heard the voice of God that day on the docks. I left for an around-the-world mission trip with Youth With A Mission (YWAM), praying that God would send me to be a missionary somewhere—anywhere in the world. Instead, at the trip's conclusion, the Lord chose to send me home, and unknown to me, Kelly was there at the Pocatello airport under a "Welcome home" banner with a large group of youth and adults from Grace Church.

While I was away on the mission trip, Kelly had transferred to Idaho State University in Pocatello to continue her studies toward her teaching credentials. The move was a bold step of faith, not knowing if I would take her back after she broke my heart.

Within four months of my return from the mission field, we were engaged to be married. She came alongside me in ministry, leading worship for our Monday-night Bible study and forming a full worship band for our Living Praise service. She still had a hard time picturing herself as a pastor's wife but had resolved to trust God with our future, believing that I was the one God had chosen for her.

I must have been lost in the moment of my recollections, because the song she was singing had ended, and all eyes in the church were on me to go up and start my message. Finding my way to the front, I prayed that the Lord would allow my mouth to speak the words that were in my heart.

"I'd like to start with a very familiar story," I began. "Many of you will remember from Sunday school the story of the wise and foolish builder. We have even sung songs about this story." To Kelly's embarrassment and awkward chuckles around the room, I broke into song:

You've got to build your house on a rock
Find a firm foundation on a solid spot
Then the rains may come and go
But the power of God you will know

"We know the story and sing with gusto about it, but we often miss the point of why Jesus told it. In this parable there were two men. One was wise and built his house on a rock; the other man was foolish and built his house on the sand. When the wind and rains of adversity hit, the wise man's house stood strong, while the foolish man's house collapsed in a pile of rubble. Now for the hundred-dollar question: What was the rock that the wise man built his house on?"

"Jesus!" a few people called out as they were used to our interactive approach.

"Sorry, this time that Sunday school answer is wrong," I replied. "Of course Jesus is the rock-solid foundation of our lives, but that's not why he told this story. What is the rock according to this story? Any other guesses?"

"The Word of God?" someone ventured to say.

"That's closer. Let's open our Bibles to Matthew chapter seven," I challenged. I asked for a volunteer to read verses 24–27. My good friend Jack stood and loudly read the passage.

> Therefore everyone who hears these words of mine and puts them into practice is like a wise man who built his house on the rock. The rain came down, the streams rose, and the winds blew and beat against that house; yet it did not fall, because it had its foundation on the rock. But everyone who hears these words of mine and does not put them into practice is like a foolish man who built his house on sand. The rain came down, the streams rose, and the winds blew and beat against that house, and it fell with a great crash.

"Now, who can tell me, what is the rock that we are to build our lives on?" I asked.

Jack was still standing as he responded, "We should not just listen to the Word of God, we need to put it into practice."

"That's absolutely right." I affirmed. "Spiritual maturity doesn't depend on how much of the Bible you know. What matters is how much of the Bible we *do*. Are we really willing to put it into practice? Some of us get deceived into thinking that we have a firm foundation because we go to church or a Bible study or memorize a few verses. When the trials of life hit, we will find out how strong our faith really is. If we have made it a lifestyle to hear the Word of God and to apply it, we find that the strength and wisdom of God's Word has been woven into the very fabric of our lives."

I continued, "But notice in this story, Jesus said that both men heard the Word. What will happen in your life if, like the foolish builder, you go to church, hear the Word, then go out and do whatever you feel like?" There was a somber muffling of responses to my rhetorical question throughout the sanctuary. "Isn't that, in essence, the definition of the foolish man? Now, I don't want you to answer this question right away, but do you think that you have been more like the wise man in the story, or more like the foolish man?" I could see serious contemplation on the faces of nearly everyone in the room.

"God has given us this beautiful gift, his Word, to teach us how to live." I held my Bible up over my head to accentuate the point. "We will be prepared for whatever life may throw at us if we make it our practice to do the Word of God. Listen to what it says in James 1:22: 'Do not merely listen to the word, and so deceive yourselves. Do what it says.' James goes on to say, 'Anyone who listens to the word but does not do what it says is like a man who looks at his face in a mirror and, after looking at himself, goes away and immediately forgets what he looks like.'

"Now you might be thinking it would take a special kind of stupid to forget what your own face looks like! It may not sound very nice, but I think that's precisely the point James is making toward professed followers of Jesus who do not follow him. James concludes this section with these words, 'But the man who looks intently into the perfect law that gives freedom, and continues to do this, not forgetting what he has heard, but doing it—he will be blessed in what he does.' Notice the repetition here, 'Do it, do it, do it.' Our faith is based on the Word of God. But it must be the Word of God that is also put into practice. We need to do it. God wants what is best for us. If only we understood the true blessing that comes from doing the Word—" I paused, letting a moment's consideration settle over the congregation.

"Jesus himself underscores this principle. In John 14:15 he says, 'If you love me, you will obey what I command.' Notice here that doing what Jesus says is an expression of love for him. In verse 21 Jesus brings this idea to its conclusion, 'Whoever has my commands and obeys them, he is the one who loves me. He who loves me will be loved by my Father, and I too will love him and show myself to him.'"

Realizing that this is the part of the message where I could start losing listeners, I asked for a volunteer. Daniel, a towheaded ten-year-old, shot his hand up in the air, so I quickly invited him up to the front. "Daniel, do you love your dad?" I could ask this question because I knew he had a great relationship with his father.

Daniel's grin widened as he looked out in the audience to find his father. "Yeah, I love my dad!"

"Okay, Daniel, I want you to be honest about this next question. Remember, your dad is listening." I paused momentarily for dramatic effect. "Do you always do what your father says?"

He looked downward with a sheepish smile and a nervous laugh. "Usually I do, but not always."

"Well, that's being very honest. Now let's pretend that your dad asked you to take out the trash and you forgot or just watched TV instead? How would your dad feel?

"He would get upset with me," Daniel replied.

"Do you know why he would feel that way?"

Daniel remained silent in thought. "Might he feel like your disobedience was a sign of disrespect, or even a lack of love?" I asked.

"I never thought of it that way," Daniel admitted.

"Now, what if your dad asked you to take out the trash while you were watching TV, and without even waiting for a commercial, you jumped up, ran to the kitchen, and took out the trash? Then when you got back you said, 'Is there anything else I can do for you, Dad?' What do you think your dad would do?"

"He would probably fall over!" Daniel giggled. The crowd enjoyed a laugh.

"He might be so pleased with you that he would reach into his pocket and give you one of these." Daniel's eyes lit up as I reached into my pocket and pulled out a crisp one-dollar bill. I handed it to him and patted him on the back. Daniel ran back to his seat waving his prize money in the air.

I looked out at the congregation. "Have you ever thought of obeying the Word of God as an opportunity to express your love for him? Jesus is longing to see that kind of response from us, and he is offering something much better than a dollar bill. Jesus is saying that our obedient love will be met with the Father's love, and that Jesus will reveal himself to us. Obedience is an invitation to intimacy with God. The more we love him, the more we will obey him, and the more we obey him, the more he will show himself to us. Isn't that the sort of intimacy our hearts are longing for?

"I want to give us all a challenge to put this word into practice. Let's go back to Matthew chapter seven, where Jesus told the story of the wise and foolish builders. He said, 'Everyone who hears these words of mine and puts them into practice.' What words was Jesus referring to?"

"The Bible," someone answered.

"Well, I believe that is correct in the broadest sense of the story. We are called to put the Bible into practice. But look at the context of this story. What particular words of his is Jesus challenging us to put into practice?" I heard the rustling of pages, so I waited.

Finally, Amy—now a senior in high school—stood up: "I have a red letter edition of the Bible where all the words of Jesus are in red print. For three whole chapters it's nothing but red. Matthew chapters five, six, and seven are all his words. Are these the words that he wants us to put into practice?"

"I think that's an excellent place to start, Amy. These chapters hold a treasury of Jesus' teachings. He talks about blessings, forgiveness, giving, prayer, fasting, worry, adultery, divorce, and many other issues relevant to our lives. Jesus concludes this collection of teachings with the story of the wise and foolish builders to encourage us to put all of his words into practice.

"I'd like to give an assignment. During the next three weeks, let's study these three chapters and keep a notebook of practical ways we can do the Word. When we meet back each Sunday, I'll give opportunity for you to report on what you are learning and doing.

"Jesus wants this to become a lifestyle for us. Not just to hear the Word of God, but to put it into practice. I'm certain that we will be challenged if we read the Bible with the idea of doing what it says. Will we just do the parts that we want to obey? How would that go over with young Daniel, for example, if he only did the chores he felt like doing? Every step of obedience is a step toward knowing God more and discovering greater intimacy with him. Let's ask Jesus to help us apply his Word."

After a reverent pause I prayed: "Lord, I know that we cannot do your Word by our own strength. We ask that you would empower us by your Holy Spirit to put the Word of God into practice. We desperately want to be closer to you and to know you better. Teach us to express our love for you by obeying your Word. Forgive us for the times when we determine for ourselves which commands we will obey and which ones we will ignore. Father, we love you and desire to express our love in obeying all your commands, no matter what the cost. In Jesus' name. Amen."

Our usual time of fellowship followed the service, with coffee and cookies and happy banter. Individuals were learning to love one another in ways that extended beyond Sunday mornings. I could hear plans in progress for groups to get together during the week. Some men spontaneously started planning breakfast Bible studies where they could talk together about putting the Word into practice.

The essence of this message would become a life passion. I had come to know Jesus as my best friend by reading the Word. Jesus had met me on the shoulder of a lonely stretch of Idaho highway and, in that hospital room, led me to a scripture that invited me to make him the Lord of my life. Jesus was teaching me to approach him with epic faith by putting the Word of God into practice. Was I now ready to obey Jesus no matter what he would require?

PART TWO

The Voice of God

Though not audible, the voice materialized, no less tangibly than actual conversation—no less real than the roughness of the wood I sat upon. The candid moment stunned me—the consideration that the Lord might actually be speaking, and to me. I remained still, trying to make sense of what I had "heard," requesting clarity or confirmation. Silence lingered.

NINE

Learning to Listen

I WALKED to the park down the street from my house, a place I often went to study my Bible. I welcomed the fresh air and warm spring sunshine after a long, cold Pocatello winter.

Several months prior, I had served on an organizational committee of church leaders that would partner with Youth With A Mission (YWAM) to bring a huge campaign to our area. As a committee member I was given a copy of the book *Is that Really You, God?* by Loren Cunningham, the founder of YWAM. In it he tells the story of his life and the birth of this evangelistic organization (which has grown into one of the largest mission agencies in the world). His book was sprinkled with examples of hearing from God and taking steps of obedience, regardless of how audacious the voice of God may seem.

I was unfamiliar with such a personal approach to following the voice of God. Although I thought I had heard the Lord's voice several times in the past, my experience was hardly that expressed by Cunningham. Perhaps due to my go-for-it personality, I came away from finishing that book thinking, *If God speaks to this Loren fellow, then certainly he can speak to me.*

This day, I had in mind to test this "hearing from God" business for myself. I spent time reading a few psalms and proverbs and preparing my heart in prayer. Finally, I began to talk to God. "Jesus, I know that you hear me when I pray, but lately I've been convicted that I don't really expect to hear from you. I know that you speak to me through the Bible, but I'd like to hear your voice. I want that kind of relationship with you in which you tell me what's on your heart. If there is anything that you'd like to say to me, I pray that you would speak to my heart now."

Before I could finish the last word, a whisper emerged in my heart and formed words in my mind, similar to the sensation of an extremely vivid idea.

"Quit your jobs, sell your house, and go to a land I will show you."

The voice seemed firm yet peaceful. But the content of the message slammed hard against my own voice of reason: This could not possibly be the voice of God. My wife has an excellent, well-paying teaching position and I'm a youth pastor. Jesus would never ask a minister to quit his job.

By this time Kelly and I had been married several years. The little house I had used as my Monday-night Bible study classroom was now a loving home. We had carved out a nice little life for ourselves. When Kelly headed off for her elementary classroom each day, I drove across town to the church every morning. We had the added pleasure of ministering together. She led worship for my youth Bible study on Monday nights and then would slip upstairs to grade papers while I walked through the Word with the young people. On Sundays she was beside me leading worship for our Living Praise service, and after that we would lead children's church together. Though far from wealthy, as "dinks" (double income, no kids) we had plenty of discretionary income and time to ourselves. We were quite comfortable.

We often talked about Grace Church as our family, where we would raise our future children and grow old together. Pastor Manfred had become like a father to me and had even expressed his desire that I take over his position at Grace when he retired. Everything seemed to be laid out perfectly. Clearly, this mysterious voice I heard in the park did not fit with our secure and well-ordered plans.

Well, that certainly didn't work, I thought with regard to my little experiment in hearing God's voice. I tried to dismiss it altogether, but it kept bugging me like an itch on the back that you can't quite reach. I finally confronted the nagging feeling. *Lord, I really wanted to hear your voice. How could you have let me down?* I decided I would give it one more try the next day. I recalled that Loren Cunningham cautioned in his book that we should "take authority over the devil" when attempting to listen to the voice of God. *That's it,* I thought. *The devil was trying to distract me with that "quit your job" business.* I would not let that happen again.

The next day I approached my quiet time in the park with renewed confidence. I took my seat atop a particular picnic table, and, after perusing some of my favorite scriptures, I resolved to listen to God. But first I remembered to take authority over the enemy: "In Jesus' name I bind the devil," I began. "Satan, you have no right or authority to speak to me, so I silence you in Jesus' name. I invite God's presence here now, and there is no space allowed for the enemy." A peace settled over me as a gentle breeze rustled budding branches overhead. Not wanting to disturb the moment, I whispered my prayer to God, "Lord, what do you want to say to me?"

The response slammed my mind with alarming clarity: "Quit your jobs, sell your house, and go to a land I will show you."

Though not audible, the voice materialized no less tangibly than actual conversation, no less real than the roughness of the wood I sat upon. The candid moment stunned me—the consideration that the Lord might actually be speaking, and to me. I remained still, trying to make sense of what I had heard, requesting confirmation. Silence lingered.

I hadn't bothered to tell Kelly about the experimental fiasco from the previous day, but now I couldn't ignore or deny that something was happening during my devotional time with Jesus, though I was not yet sure what. The conundrum distracted me the rest of that day: How would I tell Kelly about this? Would she think I was crazy?

Waiting for Kelly to return home from work, I pondered the voice.

How could I be sure it was from God? In the midst of my contemplation I was reminded of the Bible story of young Samuel hearing God's voice for the first time. Samuel's mother had dedicated him to Eli the priest to serve in the temple. The first time young Samuel heard the voice of God he mistook it for Eli's, the only father he had ever known. I smiled as I pictured little Samuel running into Eli's chambers and calling out, "Here I am! Why did you call for me?" After experiencing the same scenario several times, Eli had the wisdom to recognize that the boy was hearing the Lord's voice. "Go back to your bed," Eli instructed. "If you hear the voice calling your name again, simply say, 'Speak, for your servant is listening.'"

Pondering the familiar Bible story, the thought occurred to me: Even Samuel who became a great man of God had to learn to recognize the voice of God. He had to be taught how to listen.

The familiar sound of Kelly's Chevy Citation grinding to a halt in our driveway cut my musing short. The moment she walked in the door, book bags slung over both shoulders, Kelly instinctively knew that something was troubling me. She sat down next to me on our denim couch as I struggled to express my thoughts: "You know how I've been reading that book and thinking a lot about this idea of hearing God's voice?" I began. She listened patiently as I recounted my conversations with God over the past two mornings. I had been so reluctant to say the words that I could barely get them out of my mouth. "I mean, could it really be the Lord? What if Jesus is telling us to quit our jobs, sell our house, and go to the place he will show us?"

Kelly's response shook me and revealed the character of the woman God had chosen for me. "Well, one thing's for certain," she said, "if that really is the voice of God, then we will need to obey it."

Even as she spoke the words, I partnered with practical truth rising from deep within. I had been preaching about putting the Word of God into practice. Why should this be any different? If this was the voice of God, we needed to be no less obedient to it. But there was still that bothersome, lingering *if*. How could I be certain that the Lord was really speaking to me?

Somewhere in the quiet of the subsequent sleepless night an idea occurred to me. I had always trusted the Bible, even as a child in Sunday school: I had no doubt that the Bible was the Word of God. In high school Jesus became my best friend as he revealed himself through the stories recorded in the Gospels. While in Bible college Jesus taught me that he was the real teacher as he illuminated truth from his Word. I drifted off to sleep in peace, knowing what I must do in the morning.

As soon as Kelly went out the door and off to work, I strode down to the park by the early morning light. I tugged at my light jacket, the sun not yet warming the chilly air. My right hand gripped a well-worn leather study Bible, my faithful companion since college days. Finding my perch atop the picnic table under a massive oak tree, I felt an unexpected excitement. This time I was ready.

"Okay, Lord," I said matter-of-factly, meaning business with God. "I take authority over the enemy and silence his voice. I believe that you can talk to me so I invite you to speak, for your servant is listening."

Again the voice, now becoming more familiar, resonated in my heart. "Quit your jobs, sell your house, and go to a land I will show you."

My response revealed my expectation that he would say this again. "Lord, if that's really you, we are willing to obey. But Jesus, I need to be sure that it is you. You know that I trust this Book." I clenched my Bible and thrust it above my shoulder as if Jesus needed some visual aid to understand my speech. "You have always spoken to me through your Word. Now, if this is really your voice, I want you to say the same thing to me through the Bible."

My prayer was confident, but looking back, I'm not really sure what I expected to happen. I had never before experienced what happened next. I closed my eyes and waited patiently. Without warning, a Bible reference appeared in my mind's eye.

"Genesis 12:1–3."

This impression came as vividly and with the same firm peace I had sensed before. Still, my fingers trembled as I turned pages to the scripture I felt I was being directed to. I had no recollection of what I would find in this passage. My heart skipped a beat as I read the first verse:

The LORD had said to Abram, "Leave your country, your people and your father's household and go to the land I will show you."

I sat suspended in time as the reality of what had just happened sunk in. The Lord had clearly said the same thing to me through his Word, just as I had requested. I was stunned. What would this mean for us? My mind reeled with the ways our lives would radically change, yet I felt sure of one thing: this was God's voice and we would obey it.

Hours became like days as I waited to share with Kelly what the Lord had shown me. I decided we should meet for dinner at Dudley's, one of our favorite restaurants. I could hardly contain my excitement as our appetizers sat neglected on the table. "Can you believe it?" I said, recounting my morning event. "I opened the Bible to the place God showed me and it said the same thing as the voice I had heard. For Abram, in those days, leaving his family would have been like quitting his job, his home, and his security. Imagine what Abram must have been thinking: God didn't even tell him where he should go, he just said 'go.'" I barely stopped to take a breath. "Kelly, when I opened my Bible and read those verses from Genesis twelve, I just knew that I had been hearing the voice of God."

Kelly's excitement seemed tempered by a sober reality; I knew what she was about to say. "Marty, I trust you and believe that you've heard from God. Now we will need to obey." She swallowed hard. "But I'm scared. What will we do? What will our friends at Grace think? We don't have any plan other than saying yes to God."

"I know, honey." I tried to sound confident. "It's scary but it's also exciting. I think God is giving us an opportunity to really trust him. I think he's inviting us to come on an adventure with him, but it's one where we need to trust him for everything. What do you say? Should we go for it?"

This time her eyes twinkled. "Let's do it!" she exclaimed.

"Kel, let's commit this to the Lord right now. Let's say yes to him," I suggested. We bowed our heads to pray, reaching across our corner table at Dudley's, joining hands as we did that first time on the swimming dock at Perkins Lake. "Lord, we want you to know that we trust you. It's so uncertain what the future holds, yet we know that you will be holding us there. We commit our path to you and ask that you will lead us."

"Lord, you know what a big step this is for us and you know my own fear of letting go of control." Kelly's prayer flowed naturally from my own. "But I want you to know that I trust you more than I trust myself. I believe that you will guide us and will provide for us. We want to say yes to this faith journey you are leading us on."

Our prayers faded into excited conversation about what this step would mean for us. We lingered at Dudley's long after our meal was finished, relishing the last moments of what seemed like normalcy. One thing became certain: saying yes to God's voice was the beginning of an epic faith adventure that neither one of us could have dreamed up.

The Shepherd's Voice

NOT everyone shared our excitement about following Jesus into the great unknown.

I had scheduled a meeting with Pastor Manfred and key elders, to afford them time for our transition—toward filling the hole that Kelly and I would leave after serving the church for eight years. It was an informal setting around the dining room table at Pastor Manfred's home, but an awkward nervousness accompanied our arrival. I imagined their wondering what could be so important for Kelly and me to call this special meeting.

With great enthusiasm I launched into my story about hearing God's voice in the park, and how he confirmed it through his Word. I recounted how Kelly and I committed to following the Lord wherever he would lead. I told the group that we would finish up the academic school year at Grace, at which time I would resign.

My speech consumed all of about four eager minutes, at which time open-mouthed stares met us. Apparently, our leaders did not embrace our enthusiasm for this newly acquired fascination with God's voice. It quickly became evident that I lacked preparation for the interrogation that followed.

"What will you do after May?"

"Where will you live?"

"How will you pay your bills?"

"Are you leaving the ministry, Marty?"

We could offer only that we thought the Lord had shown us the "first step," a five-month Discipleship Training School (DTS) through Youth With A Mission.

"Well, if you want to be a missionary," Pastor offered, "why don't you go through our church denomination's board of missions? I could give you an excellent recommendation. I'm positive you would be accepted. Besides, our missionaries receive a full salary with benefits."

The invitation sounded tempting, but I could not explain why we weren't interested in considering it. When I had previously participated in missions through YWAM in Los Angeles (during the summer Kelly and I had broken up), I had traveled around the world, touching down in Germany, France, India, Thailand, and Australia. My team spent several weeks in each place, evangelizing on the streets and partnering in local mission work. It excited me like nothing I had ever experienced. The Lord impacted my life in such a profound way that I wanted to become a full-time missionary and felt drawn to do so through YWAM.

While on that trip, in Thailand, Jesus showed me a picture of returning to my church and helping Grace's people to grow in interest towards missions and practicing evangelism. At that time Jesus gave me a personal promise: *If you will be faithful to stay, Marty, many will be faithful to go.* For the past five years I had done just that, and our church had reaped plentifully. Now I sensed that it was time to go.

Despite Kelly's and my lack of long-term direction or well-laid plans, our pastor and elders said that they would give us their blessing to follow the Lord's leading. It soon became evident, however, that any discomfort they displayed came less from our choice to leave than from our claim of receiving special revelation from God.

When word finally got around that we would be leaving Grace, we faced a barrage of questions from church members and close friends. At times our answers sounded foolish even to ourselves. Jesus was calling us to quit our jobs, sell our house, and go to "only God knows where." Had we indeed "lost it" as some were suggesting? Had we really heard from God? Does God still speak to his children in such direct ways?

These doubts forced me to dig into the Bible to reconsider what the Word had to say about this idea of hearing God's voice. I went to my office desk at church, pulled out a fresh legal pad, and set it beside my Bible and exhaustive concordance. "Lord, I'm aware of what I have been taught about the dangers of extra-biblical revelation, but I also cannot deny that you have been speaking to me," I prayed. "Help me to make sense of it all. Show me what the Bible teaches about hearing your voice."

I had been learning to wait in silence and felt drawn to a memory around my parent's kitchen table. I had returned home from college during spring break, and we invited my good friend over for lunch. He had been studying to become a pastor at a denominational seminary. The topic of hearing God's voice somehow came up, and my mother surprised me by defending the idea that God still speaks to us today. My friend politely yet firmly rebuked her with his newly acquired seminary knowledge.

"Now, Milly," he began, "we can be certain that today the Lord does not speak to us except through the Bible, his written Word."

Even now I chuckle to myself remembering my mother's disarming laughter. "Oh sweetie, that's not true at all. Why, the Lord was speaking to me just this morning in my quiet time." With that, the "debate" promptly ended and we moved on to another topic.

Sitting at my desk and pondering that memory, I realized that the question of the reality of God still speaking weighed just below the surface all along. If the Bible is the visible tip of an iceberg, then the interactive communication of God is submerged beneath. Both are inseparably part of one and the same monolith of faith. Perhaps I had tried so hard to distinguish between the two—Is it the Bible, or is it the voice of God?—that I had missed the point that they are both substantive in faith, each in a way validating the other.

I had been following an arbitrary, unwritten rule: It was fine to say, "I felt the Lord nudging me" or "I sensed his prompting"—that was palatable doctrine. But to claim that Jesus had spoken to me, well, that clearly crossed the line. The voice I had heard in the park actually went beyond a nudge or prompting; it came as a command requiring a response.

"God, are you trying to tell me it's both your Word and your voice?" I inquired. "Are you still speaking to your children today in the same way as then?"

Looking down at my Bible on the desk, I began reeling mentally through it, from Genesis to Revelation, recalling my favorite Bible passages and characters. Adam, Noah, Abraham, Moses, David, Daniel, Peter, Paul, and John all had this in common: they heard and followed the voice of God. With stories looping through my mind, I picked up my Bible and held it at arm's length. "This book tells a story," I said aloud. "It's the story of God, who loves his children like a father and passionately desires to communicate with them." No sooner had I finished speaking when a Bible verse popped into my head: "Jesus Christ is the same yesterday and today and forever."

Where is that found? I thought as I flipped through the pages of my Bible. Yes, here it is, Hebrews chapter thirteen, verse eight. I read the verse again, letting it sink in. "Jesus Christ is the same yesterday and today and forever." If God is a father who speaks to his children throughout the Bible, then this verse was telling me that he hasn't changed. He still speaks today.

I took a new approach to my investigation. With my Bible and my concordance, I began researching different ways God communicated with individuals and his people in biblical times. *If God is unchanging, as it states in Hebrews 13:8, then he is able to speak to us today in the ways he spoke to us in the past,* I surmised. I recorded the following on my notepad:

The Way God Communicated	Person	Reference
Gentle whisper, still small voice	Elijah	1 Kings 19:12–13
Through a donkey	Balaam	Num. 22:21–35

Through an angel	Zechariah	Luke 1:11–13
In a dream	Joseph	Matt. 2:13
Holy Spirit guiding in truth	The disciples	John 16:12–15
Divine visitation	The disciples	John 20:19–20
An audible voice	Saul	Acts 9:1–6
Through a vision	Peter	Acts 10:9–17
Resistance by the Spirit	Paul	Acts 16:6–7
Through God's creation	All people	Rom. 1:18–20
Personal prophecies	Timothy	1 Tim. 1:18

I sat pondering my list. It was far from complete. I wondered how we could limit God to the written Word when that very communication (the Bible itself) is full of other creative ways that our Father has communicated. I was reminded of Jesus' words in John 10:27, "My sheep listen to my voice; I know them, and they follow me." I turned to that passage and realized the entire section speaks of Jesus as the Good Shepherd and of believers as his sheep. Jesus is saying that we are his sheep and we listen to his voice. I put it into my own words: "The only way Jesus can lead us step by step is if we listen to him and follow his voice."

I lowered my forehead onto my desktop and prayed, "Lord, I do believe that you are speaking to me. It doesn't matter what anyone else thinks; I want to hear your voice and commit to following you step by step."

Epic faith is an intimate longing to hear the Shepherd's voice and learn to obey it. Kelly and I would soon discover that the path Jesus leads is not always an easy one.

Stripped

MID-MAY arrived, and with the stroke of a pen it was official. Our first home now belonged to someone else, and we stood two weeks away from being jobless and homeless. It should have been a liberating start to an exciting adventure; instead we felt vulnerable and exposed.

The book of Philippians had drawn me in over the past six months. I could relate to the apostle Paul's encouragement to stay steadfast in the face of hardship and difficulty. I had read a section in chapter three so many times that I could replay it from memory:

> But whatever was to my profit I now consider loss for the sake of Christ. What is more, I consider everything a loss compared to the surpassing greatness of knowing Christ Jesus my Lord, for whose sake I have lost all things. I consider them rubbish, that I may gain Christ and be found in him, not having a righteousness of my own that comes from the law, but that which

is through faith in Christ—the righteousness that comes from God and is by faith. I want to know Christ and the power of his resurrection and the fellowship of sharing in his sufferings, becoming like him in his death. (Phil. 3:7–10)

Months earlier, I had returned to the park where I had heard God's voice so clearly. As I sat at the picnic table I'd noticed the leaves at different stages: some were still holding on to summer's green while others were dressed in brilliant yellows, reds, and oranges. Others had begun to fade, and a few had fallen lifelessly to the ground, scattered beneath my feet. Philippians chapter three lay open, capturing my attention. Out came my yellow pad and I had begun scribbling questions and reflections:

- Is knowing Jesus really the most important thing to me?
- Do I consider everything else garbage compared to being close to Christ?
- I want to know Christ and the power of his resurrection, but am I willing to be associated with his suffering?
- What does it mean to become like Jesus in his death?
- He was stripped naked, humiliated, rejected, and ridiculed as he hung on a cross.
- What does becoming like Jesus in his death have to do with knowing the power of his resurrection?

I had stared at my Bible and yellow pad while my heart pumped out more questions: Jesus, what are you trying to say to me through this passage? Why do I feel drawn to this book that talks so much about suffering? What does it mean to be stripped? The Lord was leading me down an uncertain path. I just could not get a handle on it. Perhaps the fading autumn leaves beneath my feet signaled the reality that growth and new life is often preceded by death.

YEARS earlier, long before I had heard God's voice in the park, Pastor Manfred had undergone a rather serious burnout. After years of serving the Lord with the pedal to the metal up to eighty hours a week, the wheels began to peel off. It was painful to watch this strong man who was like a father to me—someone I had viewed as an immovable rock—develop cracks that revealed vulnerable humanity. I had to double my own hectic pace to provide space for him to recover and regroup.

A new mantra had emerged whenever there was a project or program at church that needed leadership: "Marty can do it." And surprisingly, I could. In addition to youth ministries, Sunday school, adult education, and the coordination of volunteers, I took on evangelism, vacation Bible school, and an increased teaching and preaching load. I had poured all my effort into making all these ministries successful—and they were. It felt good to take on so much responsibility, and to do so with an excellence that gained the admiration of both church members and leaders. The subtle danger occurred when I began to find my identity in the success of my programs and the approval of others.

Within a year I found myself hitting an invisible wall at full speed. Just as Pastor was nearly recovered, I found that I had nothing left. Things that had run well were now falling through the cracks. I began to show up unprepared or to forget things all together. I simply could not keep up. The worst part was that I had developed some holes in my emotional bucket and even the smallest criticism or tension sapped the little strength I ran on. I was in desperate need of healing, rest, and renewal.

In response to Pastor's recommendation, or rather insistence, I developed a small group of men that provided a safety net for my fragile emotional state. I will never forget or fail to appreciate the compassion of my friends Jack, Elmer, Brad, and Randy as they allowed me to weep therapeutically in that first meeting, releasing the hurt and stress I had been carrying. With their help I began to recover some of my previous strength and endurance for the ministry, and consider new boundaries.

Both Pastor and I had been trying to keep pace with the incredible growth of our church and Christian school ministry. The announcement that Kelly and I would be moving at the end of the next year came on the heels of Manfred and me regaining some sense of normalcy.

My final nine months at Grace had started out well enough but became increasingly difficult as time wore on. I had focused my efforts on equipping others to carry out my ministry responsibilities. I would half jokingly say, "I should have been working myself out of a job all along." I was in a time of personal transition, and it felt like my position at Grace was becoming more and more like a shoe that didn't quite fit.

In my zeal to hear God's voice and follow him enthusiastically, I had made mistakes that led to misunderstandings and misinterpretations. I'd previously been regarded as a tremendous asset to our ministry and received rewards and recognition for my accomplishments up to this point. But now I felt like nothing more than a liability. It was obvious that "Marty just couldn't do it like he used to." One of the hardest blows came from the board of directors of the outdoor camp where I had invested fifteen summers of my life, extending back to my high school years. This is where my personal faith began to blossom and grow, where I had met my wife, and where I had learned leadership lessons.

Kelly and I planned to spend one last summer at the camp volunteering. My job would be building log furniture for the newly completed retreat center. The time would provide a buffer during our transition between finishing at Grace Church and taking our next step.

This was not to be. A devastating punch came in a phone call from the pastoral advisor of the camp board of directors. "The board has met and we decided to ask you not to come volunteer for the summer," the voice echoed in the receiver. Questions rang in my head as my temperature rose. While his words were sinking in, he struck the next blow. "I've been asked to inform you that you are no longer welcome to work or volunteer at the camp in any capacity. You will not be associated with our ministry in the future." The voice seemed pensive and labored; it was clearly not an easy task to deliver such news.

I tried to ask questions. What had I done? What was my offense? Was there some false doctrine I was being accused of espousing? Perhaps it was a misunderstanding that I could help clear up. No explanation was given. The decision had been made. Anger rose as I hung up the phone. "It's not supposed to be this way!" I cried out to God. "It's not fair. I don't understand. I'm just trying to follow you!"

In the weeks that followed, a low-grade fury simmered in my heart. I began to see those on the camp board as unspiritual ingrates, just as they saw me as some kind of spiritual loose cannon. Just as I was trying to recover my footing, a final blow sent me reeling.

I was shocked when church leadership called another meeting—to determine whether my employment would be terminated immediately instead of waiting the last two months until my scheduled departure date. I attended the meeting, though it seemed as if they were talking about somebody else outside the room. *This can't possibly be happening to me,* I thought.

After Jesus had spoken to me in the park and I had embraced the idea that hearing his voice and walking in obedience were vital to growing in faith, I began to reconsider my personal position on other issues, such as spiritual gifts. I had developed a friendship with one of the charismatic pastors in town and, during this difficult season, had relied on that relationship for support and understanding. I had even attended several of his church's renewal services. Through my association with this charismatic church across town, I had misrepresented my own church's doctrinal position on a number of issues. At that time, my spiritual pride kept me from seeing that I had acted inappropriately in light of my employment there.

I grew numb as church leaders discussed my situation right in front of me. Reality dropped like a bomb, and I simply could not endure it. I had been struggling to stay strong as we discussed the issues and as I tried to defend myself. In the end I simply lost it and began to weep. Yes, I had made mistakes, but did my years of faithful service and sacrifice count for nothing? This was not fair. I had previously been respected and even admired for my spirituality. Now, seemingly, I was contemptible. The assessment among trusted and lengthy relationships pierced me deeply.

The leadership announced that I would later be informed of their decision. I left the meeting numb. How could I go home and face Kelly? How could I tell her what had just happened and reveal the bleeding puncture in my heart? As I drove home, feelings of anger, bitterness, and betrayal drained what little life I had left. I must have been whitewashed when I walked in the door, because Kelly ran right to me. We collapsed onto the sofa, and through sobs I tried to explain what had just happened.

The church board informed me several days later of their decision. They would allow me to work until our originally scheduled departure, as long as I promised not to take part in any more charismatic meetings. May 31 could not come soon enough. The sting of rejection, coupled with my own feelings of defeat, broke me. I had been a young minister full of promise and potential, but now I felt branded by utter failure—a disappointment to those at the church, to myself, and certainly to God.

One day during those last few months, I hit a critical point; I didn't know whether I could keep going. I slipped out of my church office into a nearby ravine where I could hide and pour out my heart to God. I found a rock that looked out toward the foothills of Pocatello—a region of high desert Idaho that can be both beautiful and barren. Today, it mirrored my own lifelessness. "Jesus, I feel like a total failure," I cried out. "I know that I'm a disappointment to those around me, and I'm disappointed in myself. But I need to know something." My mouth quivered as I formed the words. "God, am I a disappointment to you?"

I sat on that solitary rock, listening, fully expecting that if I heard anything, it would be a rebuke from the Lord. Almost immediately, I saw in my mind's eye a memory of when I was five years old. The recollection unfolded vividly, like an old home movie of myself.

The boy's little bare feet were hurrying about the bedroom with what looked to be a very special task. He was clearing off the top of his dresser, and with great care, laying out a beautifully embroidered cloth napkin that had been used during his infant baptism. The child then carefully placed a large white candle with a blue outline of a dove and a golden cross embossed on one side upon the cloth. This candle had been used at his baptism as well and had been lit yearly on his baptismal birthday. I watched as the boy carefully added other items: a small wooden cross, his children's Bible, a picture of Jesus from Sunday school, and glow-in-the-dark praying hands. When everything was arranged perfectly at his little Jesus shrine, I watched the child take a step back and approve his work. What he did next made my eyes well up. The little boy got down on his knees with bare feet facing upward to heaven. He folded his hands like the plastic figurine. Then he bowed his head in prayer to his Father in heaven.

A tear traced my cheek as I observed the scene in my mind. It was an event from my childhood, the memory flooding back in living color. Then it happened: the voice that had spoken to me a full year ago in the park whispered not to the blond-headed boy in my mind's eye but to the broken man hidden in the barren ravine. "Marty, I'm pleased with your heart because you have given me a place. That is all I have ever wanted from you."

My tears fell like rain on dry, cracked ground. "Father, you have not been impressed by my successes or concerned about my failures; you have simply wanted my heart." In that moment, everything else was stripped away and I knelt with Jesus again, as I had so long ago on my bedroom floor. It did not matter what everyone else thought. In the Father's eyes, I was not a disappointment. God was pleased with my heart, a place long ago reserved for him, still given to him.

God-focused, epic faith compels the stripping of everything that clouds our vision so we can follow in his footsteps. Hearing God's voice again gave me the strength I needed to move forward. I knew the Father was pleased with me, and somehow only that mattered. Like the leaves that had fallen lifelessly to the ground, the Lord impressed on my heart the lesson of becoming like him, even in his suffering and death. I learned that it was not my strength but his that really mattered.

Kelly and I were two weeks away from being jobless and homeless. We had no idea where we were going, what we would do, or how we would be provided for. Yes, we felt vulnerable and exposed, even stripped of everything that we had held on to so dearly: security, respect, and the approval of others. Yet we were finding ourselves enveloped by Jesus more tangibly than we had ever known. I drew strength from the simple truth that God had shown me: he was pleased with my heart, and I would continue to give him that rightful place without reservation. It would require childlike trust in Jesus as we depended on him for each step to come.

Step by Step

I PICKED up the phone and the familiar voice of my artist friend Robert surprised me. "I heard you might be needing a place to stay." His question threw me; I was uncertain where this conversation was headed. While I stammered to gain my composure, he continued, "I know what's been going on with you and Kelly and the church. I also heard that you've sold your house. I just wanted to call and say that you and Kelly could live at my art studio while sorting out where to go from here." Robert must have heard hesitancy in my voice, which in reality was complete shock. "Don't worry, I don't want anything in return. It's absolutely free. My wife and I want you to know that we support your decision to follow Jesus, even if you don't know where you are going." God was answering prayers for our first step.

Most of our furniture had been cast-offs from folks at church. After a massive three-day garage sale, our remaining belongings fit on top my friend Steve's truck and flatbed trailer. He kindly helped us deliver our possessions to Robert's art studio several hours away. We quickly realized that our previous perception of "art studio" was an ill-painted picture. We arrived to a beautiful two-story log cabin atop a grassy hill beside a secluded stretch of the massive Snake River. Kelly and I sensed Jesus' smile while we were beginning to learn how to walk by faith.

We had no idea that the Lord would open this door and provide a stunning, restful place for us to live. It blossomed into a quiet season of healing and restoration for us. Several friends admired the log furniture that I had built as a hobby, and now commissioned me to build pieces for their own homes. This would provide a meager income for Kelly and myself in this transition time, and I gladly agreed.

I had not realized the toll the previous years had taken on me, and found myself content building furniture in solitude for hours on end. I began harboring the idea that God was finished with me in ministry, and I thought I would never preach again. It seemed fine with me, really, since I had come to realize my identity was not in what I did but rather in my relationship with Jesus. Spending days shaping rough logs into artistic pieces of furniture, I often thought about how Jesus must have worked with his father Joseph in the carpentry shop. If it was good enough for Jesus, then who was I to complain if God wanted me to spend the rest of my life working with wood?

I took lunch breaks at noon with Kelly, enjoying the view from the cabin's front deck. After these leisurely meals together, I would return to my makeshift shop in Robert's shed for the remainder of the afternoon. When finished for the day, I doused away the sweat and sawdust with a brisk dunk in the irrigation canal that flowed through the front yard. What a refreshing feeling to work with my hands—creating items both beautiful and useful. My tension and stress began to melt, replaced by peace and wholeness.

I was also rediscovering my relationship with Kelly, the love of my life. In full-time ministry, the ones you care about sometimes get leftovers. This reprieve began to remind me again of my foremost ministry—my family.

In the evenings, we enjoyed simple dinners. Occasionally for dessert we walked to the gas station two miles down the road and got ice cream bars before taking the long stroll home. It seemed a short jaunt as we held hands, conversing all the way. "Kel, these days it seems like all we have left is each other," I said one evening as we strode along. "Each other and Jesus, I should say."

"With you, Marty, if Jesus is all we have, then Jesus is all we need," Kelly responded without hesitation. It became a motto for us in the years that followed: "When Jesus is all you have, Jesus is all you need."

We would relax on the back porch and watch the sun setting over the river below. Our conversation often drifted to the next step that God would have for us. Apparently, God was teaching us to walk by faith, showing us only one footfall at a time. God had commanded us to quit our jobs and sell our house. We did that. Then God opened the door through Robert's invitation to live at his studio. Having taken that step, we anticipated that the Lord would then reveal to us "the land I will show you" part—confirming our next move to do a Discipleship Training School with YWAM.

One evening Kelly broke out into prayer. "Lord Jesus, we need your direction. Show us the next step. We believe that you are leading us to attend a DTS, but where? Please guide us to the place you've chosen for us."

Within days, my sister Julie called and suggested that we meet her family in Denver, Colorado. They had planned to make the drive from Kansas and urged us to come down from Idaho, meeting them in the middle. "Marty, you could go to the Promise Keepers rally with Gary and some of the men from our church, and Kelly could hang out with me and my friends," she prodded. "Besides, we haven't seen you for a while—it'll be fun."

"Let's do it, Kel!" I exclaimed after my conversation with Julie. "We've been wondering about the YWAM locations in Denver and Colorado Springs. This trip would give us opportunity to visit those bases and could help us make a decision." We were open to hearing God's voice about which training base to attend, but I figured a little research would not hurt.

T H E atmosphere at the Promise Keepers rally was electric. I found myself worshiping Jesus in Denver's Bronco Stadium with sixty thousand other men who desired a closer walk with him. I could sense my spirit being lifted and filled with renewed vision. And I was confident that God had brought me to this very place. After our lunch break I became separated from my brother-in-law Gary and his group and had to find a place to sit by myself. Pastor Jack Hayford riveted my mind as he addressed us on the issue of submitting our life choices to the Lord. I felt I was the only person in the stadium and he was speaking directly to me.

"Go ahead and meet the person in front or behind you," Pastor Hayford instructed as he concluded his message. "Tell that person about the choices in your life that you need to submit to the Lord, and pray together, asking for God's direction."

The obvious thing on my mind was our next step: where to go for a DTS. Kelly and I had visited the Denver base and although the property and people were amazing, we were not sensing a strong pull there. Our next visit would be in two days, to YWAM in Colorado Springs, but how could we be sure if God wanted that? I turned around and was greeted by two vibrant men in their early thirties, just like myself.

"Hi, I'm Jim, and this is my friend Wes," said the friendly man with blue eyes and brown wavy hair, pumping my hand vigorously. "We both work with a missions organization nearby," he continued.

"Really? Which mission organization are you a part of?"

"Have you ever heard of Youth With A Mission?" Wes inquired.

I could hardly contain my excitement. "Yes, of course. Which YWAM base are you guys from?"

"From the one in Colorado Springs," Jim offered.

Their astonishment joined my own when I said, "My wife and I are scheduled to visit your base this Tuesday. That's the life choice I was going to share with you: which YWAM base does God want my wife and I to attend for our DTS?"

The three of us marveled at the Lord's guidance as we bowed in prayer to thank him for the answer even before we uttered the question. Out of sixty thousand men packed into a football stadium, the Lord had allowed me to lose my group so I could meet two men whom God used to encourage me. Kelly and I were on the right track. Our visit to YWAM Colorado Springs two days later confirmed what the Lord was speaking to us. This would be our next step.

DURING the first week of our DTS, we got to know the staff and fellow students and pictured what we could expect in the weeks and months to come. As we came to know those at the base, it was obvious that they loved Jesus. We heard stories similar to ours, of leaving everything, selling everything, just to follow Jesus with all their hearts. Kelly and I also learned more about what it meant to really trust Jesus. None at YWAM received a salary from the organization. They each had to raise their own support in order to focus all of their time and energy on missions. It was evident that these YWAMers had a passion to make the name of Jesus and his message of salvation known throughout the world.

Yet despite this exciting atmosphere for growth, something held me back that I could not put my finger on. During that week I had heard about a men's meeting at one of the local churches and decided to attend.

"Some of us as men are wearing a ball and chain around our leg," I overheard the speaker say as I slipped into the back of the meeting already in progress. "That ball and chain is called anger, and some of you don't even know it's there. You are trying to walk in the footsteps of Jesus, but every time you take two steps forward you trip over the chain again. Tonight we are going to learn to deal with anger through the power of forgiveness."

In that moment God's still, small voice confirmed what I already knew in my heart as true: "Marty, this message is for you. Your anger toward the camp board and the church leaders is holding you back. You need to forgive them." My face flushed red and my heart pumped; I had been found out. Anger was lodged in the recesses of my heart; I had given it a foothold. This confrontation made my heart scream, "No!"

"God, you can't expect me to just forgive them. I was hurt. I was treated unfairly. I demand an apology; then I'll consider forgiving them." Even in my prayer, anger reared its ugly head. I closed my eyes to shut out what I was being forced to consider, but instead a picture of a cross confronted me. Darkness veiled the figure that hung upon it, but the voice rang out loud and clear.

"Father, forgive them. They know not what they do."

My heart melted as all my arguments toppled lifelessly to the ground. "Jesus, you were betrayed. You were mocked. You were stripped, and hung naked on a cross, broken and empty. No one apologized for what they had done to you, yet you forgave."

"Marty, I want you to forgive and write a letter of apology."

Even though I admitted I bore some responsibility for the painful ending of our time at Grace, the idea that I should apologize came as a complete shock. I had rationalized that I carried less than ten percent of the blame; my mistakes could not possibly justify the wrong that I had incurred. The words stung, but how could I argue with the one who had endured so much, yet had the heart to forgive? I recalled a Bible verse from Philippians that said: "Jesus humbled himself and became obedient even to death on the cross." Perhaps healing comes by taking a humble position, I thought.

I slumped back in my chair and conceded to the truth of what must be done. Even before the men's meeting was over, I slipped out and found my pickup in the parking lot. I drove to the top of a hill where I could see the city lights sprawling out for miles. I found a yellow pad behind the seat and humbly began writing letters of apology and forgiveness to leaders who had hurt me.

I completed the project after midnight. It felt liberating. It occurred to me that the voice of God was teaching me lessons of epic faith that I had never before considered. The problem, though, was that by morning light I would lack the courage to mail them.

WICK, a regional leader for YWAM, spoke the following week at our DTS. Short in stature with a dark, bushy mustache, he exuded something inviting. He spoke powerfully on the topic of our destiny being rooted in relationship with God and others. His teaching was delivered with the authority of Jesus. On the last day of class I realized why.

"I want you to know that I've been praying for each one of you throughout the week," Wick proceeded. "Often, Jesus gives me words for you during my prayer times. I'd like to spend time this morning just praying for you." Kelly and I watched in amazement as he called up our classmates one by one and prayed for them. We had never experienced prophetic prayer before, but as Wick prayed, the expressions on our classmates' faces revealed that he was ministering with revelatory words that had obviously been given by Jesus.

"Next, I'd like to pray for Marty and Kelly," I heard him announce. I grew nauseous as we settled into two chairs that faced the classroom. I had thought it fine for him to practice prophetic prayer over others but was not yet comfortable receiving this sort of thing, especially with spectators. My discomfort went through the roof when this man of God dropped onto his knees, and with his face on the floor, grabbed hold of my feet. Straightaway my inhibitions quickly faded when he gazed upward, deep into my eyes, tears filling his own.

"Marty, Jesus wants me to tell you something," Wick announced in an utterly sincere tone. "I myself am a leader. On behalf of leaders who have hurt you, I beg for your forgiveness." His head descended over my feet again and he wept, broken with contrition—identifying with the pain that other leaders had caused.

The dam of my heart broke, flooding my eyes. Kelly tightly gripped my hand. My mouth opened and its wailing echoed off the classroom walls. Every last bit of pain—with its anger and resentment—drained from me, replaced by a transcending peace. Kelly's tears mingled with my own as deep healing occurred in both of us. The bitterness harbored in our hearts was displaced by the tangible presence of Jesus.

As soon as our prayer time ended, I went out and found the apologies I'd written, tucked behind my pickup seat. I plunked them into the nearest mailbox, realizing that I had just taken an epic step of faith. Forgiveness. I was free.

"KEL, it's only the third week of our school but it seems that we've already learned a lifetime of lessons," I marveled as we sat in bed doing our reading assignments for the week.

"Yeah, I know. I just don't know how much more spiritual stretching I can take," she responded jokingly while glancing over her book.

"Do you ever wonder what's next? I mean, this school will be over before we know it—then what? Do you think we'll go back to Robert's place where I can keep building furniture, or—?" My thoughts trailed off, not wanting to get my hopes up that perhaps the Lord still had plans to use me in ministry.

"I'm sure God has something terrific in store for us," she responded, sensing my apprehension. "Let's keep praying that he will show us the next step.

"MARTY and Kelly, I wanted to talk with you because I've sensed the Lord putting you on my heart this entire week." We felt privileged to be having a special meeting with Dave, the guest speaker, but frankly were quite curious as to where this was heading. "Let me just get to the point: At my YWAM base in Los Angeles we run a missions program for youth. You see, the kids come with their youth pastor as a group, but it really runs more like a camp." I could feel Kelly's eyes darting toward me now and again as Dave spoke, but I didn't want to miss a single word. "We equip the groups with tools for evangelism and creative arts, and then we send them on a week-long mission trip. I have no idea if you have any experience in camp ministry, or youth ministry, or teaching or taking groups on mission trips, but I feel like Jesus is telling me to invite you to come and lead this program. Does this sound like something you would be interested in?"

Already Kelly and I shared a knowing look, and wondered who should be the first to share our qualifications with Dave. As Kelly spoke of our past experience, hope was building—perhaps the Lord was not finished with us after all. Could it be that everything we had done in the past had prepared us for this next step?

I recalled the Mission Camp program we had tried to develop back in Idaho.

I'd had a grand vision to use Camp Perkins as a base of operation for a program to train youth for short-term mission trips. In fact, only two weeks after our honeymoon, Kelly and I traveled to rural Mexico with a team of high school students on our first outreach. After a week of recovery, we led a second outreach to Utah. I had big plans for Mission Camp, but in the end, the camp board shut it down, citing it outside the primary purpose of the camp's ministry. My disappointment was palpable. I had to let the vision die.

But now, sitting across from us, Dave seemed equally impressed that our past experiences had uniquely prepared us for the opportunity he presented. He was careful to warn that regardless of how good the fit seemed to be, we needed to pray and seek the word of the Lord as to whether this was God's leading. In the meantime, he would discuss the matter with the leaders at his base.

I was a bit taken aback by Dave's use of the phrase "the word of the Lord." I had always thought that phrase referred to the Bible itself. A quick study revealed that when the Bible uses the phrase "the word of the Lord," it usually refers to the voice of God, such as "The word of the Lord came to Jeremiah." After spending focused time in prayer, Kelly and I were confident that we had the word of the Lord to accept Dave's invitation to go on staff with YWAM Los Angeles. This would become our next step after our overseas DTS outreach phase was complete. We could not wait to call and let Dave know that we had reached a decision.

The next morning, I found myself lying awake in bed before the sun came up. I could not stop wondering how it would feel to lead such a big missions program. What would it be like to live in Los Angeles? *I guess the Lord still has a plan to use me in ministry.* With Kelly asleep beside me, I heard that familiar voice in my heart:

"Marty, this will be your mission camp. It is a dream I am giving back to you."

Jesus was teaching us to walk in faith by revealing only the next step we were to take. Epic faith necessitates obedience to Jesus one step at a time on the journey that he has mapped out for us. The road ahead would require us to trust him in ways we had never experienced before.

THIRTEEN

Dependent on God

KELLY held up a handful of unstamped envelopes as she cried out to God, "We need you to come through for us. God, we are doing this for you and we don't even have enough money to put postage on these newsletters. God, this is your responsibility. If you want us to continue as missionaries, we need you to provide for us."

I squeezed Kelly's hand as she prayed, but found it difficult to muster faith in that moment. We were fatigued from trusting God for every little thing. We knew that each step of our missionary lifestyle would require us to walk by faith, but we had no idea how absolutely dependent on God we would become. Within a year of joining staff with YWAM Los Angeles, we began to question if we were really cut out for this. Might we actually give up over the lack of one hundred stamps? This predicament was reminiscent of the first support letter we had sent, except now hope had been displaced by the weight of circumstances.

OUR Discipleship Training School in Colorado Springs went on a three-month outreach to Turkey. Our team spent months rebuilding and repairing homes devastated by a flash flood. Through acts of service we earned the right to share our hope in Jesus Christ. On one occasion, we shared the gospel through drama in front of a restored home. All of the neighbors had assembled, watching intently when police cars suddenly roared up to the home with sirens blaring. (Openly preaching the gospel is a criminal offense in this country.) The eldest son of the family we had served boldly approached the police and told them to get back in their cars. "Leave these people alone," he said. "They are our friends and we are hosting a party in their honor." Remarkably, the officers returned to their cars and drove away. Another time we preached the gospel in a crowded open market. A local Imam approached us after we finished. Rather than reprimanding our group, the Islamic leader invited us to come to his mosque. In private, he asked us to pray for him and his wife, as they had remained childless for years. He had observed how we had served the people in his community and had heard that we had prayed for the sick with miraculous results. Even after we left the country, we continued to pray that the seeds we planted would have a lasting impact.

Through these experiences, Kelly and I felt like we had transformed into real life missionaries. Our next step of joining YWAM full-time required us to raise a monthly financial support team of our own. We had paid for our DTS and the outreach to Turkey out of profits from the sale of our house back in Pocatello. Our dwindling reserves made us face the reality that to continue on with YWAM we would need to begin the humbling task of asking for money.

We found ourselves back at Robert's cabin preparing to relocate to Los Angeles. Kelly and I had written a letter asking for monthly support and we were busily stuffing envelopes and addressing them.

"I wonder if this is what Peter felt like," I said.

"What do you mean?"

"Well, you know the story where the disciples see Jesus walking on water and Peter says, 'If it's really you, Lord, then invite me to come walk on the water with you?'"

"Yes, but what does that have to do with us?" Kelly asked.

"How did Peter know the water would hold him? I mean, everyone knows that water can't hold you up, but sure enough, Peter stepped out of the boat and started walking on the water. I guess I'm feeling like Jesus is inviting us to step out of the boat, but I'm not sure the water can hold us."

"It's not the water we need to trust. It's him," Kelly mused. "Remember, Peter started to sink the moment he took his eyes off Jesus."

"You're right about that," I admitted. "We're going to have to keep our eyes fixed on Jesus every step of the way to keep from drowning."

"It feels scary to me too, to be so completely dependent on Jesus," Kelly confessed. "But that's silly, if you think about it. Who is more able and trustworthy than him?"

"I guess it's God's responsibility to take care of us, if he's the one calling us to be missionaries. It's Jesus who's calling us out of the boat to follow him; it will be up to him to provide for us," I said, still not entirely sure I believed my own words.

"That's the last of them," Kelly announced, admiring a large stack of envelopes. "How about you step out of the boat and run these down to the post office?"

In short time the replies began to roll in, but none hit us more profoundly than the one addressed from Pastor Manfred and his wife. Kelly and I had felt unsettled about our strained relationship with them due to our difficult departure from Grace Church. We had prayed that as a sign of God completing the work of forgiveness and of restoring our friendship, they would willingly join our financial support team—a most improbable request considering that they never approved of us joining YWAM to begin with.

"You open it," Kelly urged as she shoved the letter into my hands.

I ripped open the envelope and found the response card, with a marked commitment to support us monthly, along with a short handwritten note: "May God richly bless you on your next step in ministry." The brief words were far more precious than the pledged amount of money. God was restoring our relationship.

God had invited us to step out of the boat, and I could feel the water becoming firm beneath my feet. Within a few months we had enough financial pledges to make our way to LA in a rented U-Haul truck.

Kelly and I found it curious that YWAM missionaries we had met told similar stories of how God provided miraculously for them. I never imagined that God would work miracles for us. It had never occurred to me that the reason so many YWAM missionaries see the Lord working miracles on their behalf is that their lives completely depend on it.

Within our first few months in Los Angeles, we discovered that half of our initial monthly pledges would never materialize. Now we were like everyone else, believing God for literally everything. We had enough to give our tithe, pay our base fee (which provided basic food and housing), and pay our auto insurance—that was it. If we needed dish soap or toothpaste, we had to pray for it.

Our YWAM ministry had a weekly food distribution. As a local nonprofit, YWAM LA received a regular allotment of damaged goods and expired products from another local charity. At a set time on Fridays, all the items were laid out on tables and the YWAM staff could rummage through it and take what they needed. The funny thing about "distribution" is that you never knew what you might find. Kelly started the practice of making a weekly shopping list knowing full well that we could not afford to buy anything on it. If we had run out of deodorant, shampoo, or Q-tips, it would go on the list. Then we would pray over that list, asking God to provide.

Distribution became an exciting scavenger hunt to see how God would answer our prayers. Kelly and I would pick through boxes of miscellaneous goods and each week found the exact items matching her list. At times the needs were so specific that such a "find" bordered on the impossible. I was skeptical, for instance, when she listed a pregnancy test and boxed hair color by brand and number. But sure enough, they materialized the next week. When others learned of our shopping prayer list, they would help us look for some of the improbable items. The discoverer would whoop and holler, waving the item in the air, "Here it is, Kelly. I found it!" Like a game, we began to do the same thing for other missionaries who in turn started making their own distribution prayer lists.

Kelly and I began calling this season our manna years because, like the children of Israel walking in the desert, God provided only what was needed and only when needed. No surplus remained, but there was always enough.

Whether we have little or abundance, epic faith requires dependency on God.

IN SPITE of all the encouraging little miracles, we endured relentless stress living hand-to-mouth and trusting God for every little thing. Perhaps our fatigue grew from several years of being so downright dependent on God, but that pile of letters represented a breaking point for both Kelly and me. Neither one of us spoke as we walked hand in hand down the hot sidewalk to the base mailroom to see if God would somehow miraculously supply our need. We did not want to voice what we knew we both were thinking: Are we really called to be missionaries? What if God does not provide? Should we give up, go back, and get "real jobs"?

The YWAM mailroom would receive a daily canvas mailbag, and Suzanne, a staff member, was responsible to sort it into boxes reserved for each missionary or family. At times we received a card from a friend or relative, sometimes containing a small gift of support. "You go check," Kelly said as she nudged me toward the mailroom. I sensed her aversion to the disappointment of an empty mail slot, so I acted bravely as I tugged the door open. I immediately noticed that all the boxes were empty; the mail had not yet arrived. Nevertheless, I reached up to run my hand through our mail slot, and my fingers brushed against something unseen, lying flat. I carefully slid it out and found a plain sealed envelope with a simple handwritten inscription: *For Marty & Kelly.* I immediately tore it open to find thirty-three dollars in cash. No note or explanation was given, nor needed. We had not informed a single person about this need, yet God had provided exact postage for one hundred 33-cent stamps.

I shook as I walked from the mailroom through an adjacent door to the campus bookstore. I discovered Suzanne there, looking out the window, expecting the postal truck to arrive.

"Hey, Suzanne, can I get one hundred stamps from you?" I said confidently as I pulled thirty-three dollars from the envelope. I tried to play it cool when I returned to the breezeway where Kelly had waited, but I had to bite my lip when I approached her with a roll of stamps in one hand and an empty envelope in the other. Kelly's eyes flashed with an obvious question, but I could respond only with tears. The envelope and stamps told the story, and overcome with emotion, we both began to simultaneously laugh, cry, and pray.

"Father, we are so sorry for doubting you. You have always been faithful and have blessed us beyond anything we deserve. Don't ever let us forget what an honor and a privilege it is to be your missionaries. Thank you for providing for us. Thank you for postage stamps. We trust that you will always take care of us."

TRUSTING God to meet our needs became a way of life. When we lacked money to pay our bills, we would remind ourselves (and God) that it was his responsibility to take care of us.

Once, we had a problem with the passenger window on the driver's side of our car, stuck halfway down. I took it to the Toyota dealership to find that the motor had failed and would cost over $300 to replace. That exceeded what we had, so we just drove around with it that way: a real hassle when it rained, and a safety hazard in LA. Yet, when getting ready to leave for a two-week trip, we felt that it was poor stewardship to leave our car sitting unattended in that condition. I resolved to have the window fixed, paying by credit card, something I was not comfortable doing since we did not have the money to pay off the card. As we were leaving for the Toyota dealership, Kelly had to stop at the base mailroom to send off a package. She ran in while I sat in the car stewing about having to pay money we did not have to fix a dumb car window. In the most unexpected way I heard the Lord's voice in my heart say, "Why don't you pray for the window?"

I immediately became self-conscious and looked around to see if anyone was watching. How silly would that be, to pray that God would heal my car? Yet the voice had tugged at my heart; I knew Jesus wanted me to take a clear step of faith outside my comfort zone.

My hand trembled as I reached for the panel that controlled the power windows. "Lord, I know that you can do all things, even heal my car window," I prayed aloud as I touched the button that controlled the broken window. "Because you asked me to pray for it, I ask that you would heal this window now in Jesus' name. Amen."

I pushed the button toward the up position. I nearly jumped out of my skin as the motor hummed and the window slid up into place. It felt like the presence of God entered that car to move the window himself.

Kelly returned and immediately noticed the window back up, then incredulously asked what had happened.

"G-God," I stammered, "he healed the window, but don't touch it! Now that it's up, let's leave it alone." And we did. We did not touch that control button for months. Finally, my buddy Wayne confronted me.

"Didn't you tell me how God healed your window?"

"Yes. Wasn't that a crazy amazing miracle?"

"Well, why don't you use it then? Don't you think if God healed your window he would make it so that it could go up and down?"

Wayne certainly had a perceptive point, and despite the obvious nature of the miracle, I stood guilty of both unbelief and of not giving God credit for completely fixing it.

"You're right, Wayne. Let's try it." I pressed the button and it went down. I pressed it again and it went back up. We operated that button like two giddy schoolboys as we sped along Interstate 210.

By hearing God's voice and taking steps of obedience, Kelly and I were becoming discipled in absolute dependence on God. We were also discovering that he is a faithful Father who delights in providing everything from postage stamps to car repairs. We were like excitable children walking with the Father daily by faith. We would soon be on an adventure that would require us to depend on him for every little step—literally.

FOURTEEN

Backpacking

EVER since my high school years, my brother Rob and I had taken annual week-long backpacking adventures with some of our closest friends through the mountains of Idaho. When God called Kelly and me into missions, I realized that these excursions would have to be surrendered to him. Summertime, when our annual backpack trips were scheduled, was now our most demanding season, training and coordinating mission trips for over a thousand youth. Going on the annual "Big Trip" with my brother and buddies was not an option.

At the close of one particular summer, I prayed, "Father, I know that you are good and you love to give your children the desires of their hearts. I would be so grateful if you somehow worked out a way for me to enjoy a backpacking trip again." After uttering this simple request one morning during my quiet time, I forgot about it. But God did not.

Several weeks later, walking through the parking lot at the YWAM base, John, the LA Discipleship Training School leader caught my attention. "Hey Marty, do you want to go to Nepal?" he blurted out.

I gave him a big questioning smile as if to say, "What in the world are you talking about?"

John continued, "We have a DTS outreach scheduled to go to Nepal, but our outreach leaders aren't able to go. If I can't find someone that I trust to lead it, I'll have to cancel the whole outreach. How about you and Kelly? Would you want to lead it?"

Stunned, I replied, "Are you serious? You want us to take a team to Nepal? When?"

"The outreach leaves in a month. We have to make a final decision this week whether it's a go."

"I'll have to talk to Kelly about it," I responded, but inwardly I was thinking she'd never go for it.

My head was still reeling from the conversation as I walked through our front door. We lived on base property in half of a doublewide trailer, the other half filled with single guy staff. We had lovingly made it home. "Guess who I ran into in the parking lot?" I began. "John cornered me and wants us to lead the DTS outreach to Nepal; can you imagine that?"

"Well, did you tell him yes?"

I looked at Kelly to see if she was kidding, but I gazed into her determined expression and realized she was serious. Between the two of us, Kelly is the cautious one, while I am more impulsive. *Who is this woman?* I thought.

Kelly interpreted my shock. "You know we've been talking about wanting to go on another overseas outreach. We haven't really been on the field since Turkey. I think we should go for it."

"Okay, let's pray about it right now." I blurted out, not wanting to abort Kelly's grand moment of spontaneity. "Jesus, we don't want to take a step to the left or right apart from your direction, so we ask you to speak into this decision. Do you want Kelly and I to lead this outreach to Nepal?"

We began to wait silently for the Lord's response. I was reminded of a prophetic word given to me less than a month prior. I had been ministering with my friend Dan in the Seattle area when Junior, a Samoan friend of mine, suggested, "Hey bros, I want to take you to see Victor the prophet. He's my bro from Puerto Rico. You will be so blessed by him." I was initially reluctant because of my church background; anyone with "prophet" in his or her name should naturally be met with suspicion. Dan and I agreed to go and meet Victor in spite of my reservation and found him to be a pleasant older gentleman with a thick accent. It all seemed quite normal until Victor announced that he was going to pray for us and Junior turned on a tape recorder as if on cue.

"I see that the Lord's a-gonna change-a your plans," Victor began in drawn out resonating syllables, eyes closed, left hand placed gently on my back. "You think-a that your a-gonna go this way, but the Lord's a-gonna send you that way. I see ya away far off a-preachin' the gospel in a distant land. And the Lord he wants ya to know that there's a-two that are walkin' beside ya. Ya need not fear cause they're always-a with ya."

Okay, that was weird, I thought. But as hard as I tried, I could not dismiss Victor's words.

So as Kelly and I awaited the Lord's direction about Nepal, it occurred to me that I needed to change my January plans. I had hoped to arrange to travel and speak at some churches and youth groups, but I would have to reschedule that to go to Nepal. Perhaps these strange words from a Puerto Rican prophet were part of the Lord's divine guidance preparing our "yes" to an unexpected directional change.

Kelly squeezed my hand and said, "I feel like Jesus is saying, 'Do not be afraid.' He will be with us as we go to Nepal."

I smiled broadly, "I got a yes too."

I could not wait to tell John. I picked up the telephone and made the call.

"John, we're in."

"What do you mean?"

"Kelly and I prayed about it. We want to lead the DTS team to Nepal!"

"That's great," he said, then added, "Oh, I forgot to tell you earlier, this is a backpacking outreach in the Himalayas—are you and Kelly okay with that?"

The phone receiver just about hit the floor before I stammered, "Uh, th—that will be fine with us."

A backpacking outreach. The Lord had remembered my prayer.

THE first day of backpacking required a helicopter flight into our trailhead. We had scheduled a short shuttle from Pokhara to Jomsom, where we would begin our trek, but for days fog had buried Jomsom. After several days of delay, Royal Nepal Air decided to call in an old army helicopter for the job. Our team of eight loaded onto the benches inside the chopper with a half dozen other passengers and everyone's gear. We held our breath and our packs up against our knees as rotors cranked against thin air, struggling for lift. The hovering beast tilted and began its climb through a narrow valley into the Himalayan range. Although enduring cramped quarters in a drafty, non-pressurized craft, I was thankful to be jammed next to a small round window. As the vessel climbed, the magnificent mountain peaks, Annapurna and Machapuchare, emerged in breathtaking view. I could not believe that soon I would actually trek the Himalayas.

My excitement dampened upon piling out of the helicopter, as my wife made a beeline for the nearest wall to vomit behind. The rarified ride, while thrilling me, had spiraled her into motion-induced altitude sickness. Kelly lay on the ground resting while the team members readied their gear. It wasn't long, however, before John, our Nepalese trekking guide, began to press us onward. "We must get going. It is a long way to Kagbeni. We must arrive there before nightfall."

John, a believer, had dedicated his life to sharing Jesus with others. He and his wife founded an orphanage, taking in abandoned children, caring for them, and teaching them to be followers of Jesus. He exuded joy through a contagious laugh, but he also proved to be a real go-getter. His prodding convinced us to start moving.

I could see that Kelly was trying to be valiant. She insisted on walking, but hauling her backpack in her weakened state would be impossible. My backpack weighed-in heavier than any I'd ever carried; the entire bottom compartment held gospel literature. While in Kathmandu, I discovered a Bible society and purchased from them as many full-color, illustrated Nepali Gospel of John booklets as I could carry. At that time, the distribution of gospel literature was illegal, so I concealed the booklets in that huge compartment. Our Nepalese trekking guide expressed excitement because no gospel literature, to his knowledge, had ever been distributed in the region that we would trek. Yet he cautioned us to be very careful.

I took hold of Kelly's pack, and by turning it upside down, managed to buckle its waist strap around the top of my own cumbersome load. Then I cinched her pack's shoulder straps to the bottom, mating the two into one behemoth pack. I could not lift it myself, so two guys from our team hoisted it into place. I tightly fastened my belt and shoulder straps and leaned forward to manage the mass. Hiking with this load proved laborious, but I considered that I had it easy compared to Kelly, who was still reeling with frequent rounds of sickness.

The chalky rocks rattled with each step as John navigated us through the boulders of the dry Kali Gandaki riverbed. We then ascended toward cold blue skies on a stark, narrow trail that eventually deposited us at the Kagbeni village gates. We found a small trekking lodge and I could hardly wait to be released from my behemoth burden. I dropped my pack at the front desk with a thud. After making arrangements for our team to stay the night, the owner reached for my pack saying, "Now I show you to your rooms." Our team smirked knowingly when the pack did not budge. The lodge owner repositioned himself and put both arms into the effort, but the pack never left the floor. He released his grip, and smiling broadly he looked at me, "You: Sherpa." I took it as the highest compliment, being associated with the region's porters who haul heavy loads over mountaintops and up Mount Everest itself. Kelly was able to shoulder her own pack for the rest of the trip, but that never stopped our team members from calling me "Sherpa."

Kelly and the team wanted to rest and remain at the lodge while dinner was being prepared. I, on the other hand, could not wait to explore the sights. As I approached the city's west gate I noticed above the road a yellow sign with red lettering. Written in both Nepali and English, it warned: RESTRICTED MUSTANG REGION—NO ENTRY WITH-OUT PERMIT. I had read about the Mustang, the people who lived in this area. No known believers existed among them. I had prayed for these people with such conviction, and now I was so close. I felt a wave of faith rising up in me, desiring to pray for them on their own soil.

I slipped several steps past the sign to enter the Mustang region. "Lord Jesus, I pray for the Mustang people and this region where they dwell. I pray that these gates may be opened for the gospel to flood into this place. Just as Joshua claimed your promise that you would give him every place where he set his feet, so I am claiming the Mustang region for Jesus." As I prayed, I reached down and grabbed a handful of dry dirt and continued, "Father, even as I stand here, I call forth your missionaries to bring your gospel to this dry and needy land. Send the seeds of the gospel and water them with the reign of your Holy Spirit, in Jesus' name. Amen."

I worked my way back toward the trekking lodge, energized by praying for the Mustang, but soon happened upon a Buddhist monastery. A sign at the monastery gate surprised me: VISITOR'S ENTRANCE FEE: 40 RUPEES. Checking my watch, I realized that visiting hours had passed, but I called out anyway.

"Hello. Is anyone there?"

After a brief time, a toothless, cross-eyed monk peered down from an upper balcony. I quickly realized that he understood no English, so in signs and gestures I tried to communicate that I wanted to enter. Finally he recited, "Forty rupees," and motioned for me. The monk leveraged open the stout wooden door and led me up a dark stone staircase by the light of a single oil lamp. I handed him two twenty-rupee notes and he pulled back a thick velvet curtain, revealing an inner chamber glowing by the combined light of what seemed like a thousand candles. He led me in and I noticed ornate wall carvings, and in the front of the chamber, a massive golden Buddha. I marveled at the beauty of this inner chamber and at the same time sensed therein a dark and oppressive spirit.

A constant deep drumming resounded from a distant chamber and so I inquired. The monk must have understood my charade-like query. Through a toothless wide grin, he proudly answered, "Lama." I had studied Buddhism and understood some of the dark and demonic practices of this seemingly benign religion. I knew that somewhere in this monastery the lama was leading a hypnotic chanting ritual with the beat of this drum.

I am not sure how long I remained in the room—I felt caught in a timeless flashback from the *Kung Fu* TV series. Eventually roused by the monk motioning my departure, I again felt a wave of faith rising up inside me. Through gestures I struggled to communicate that I needed a few more minutes to pray in this place, and he showed approval, thinking I intended to pray to his god, not against it.

I knelt down in the cold, flickering chamber and began to pray softly in the Spirit. When I perceived the Lord stirring my heart, I spoke aloud, "Jesus, I pray that your glorious light would shine in this place. These people are held in the dark bondage of the enemy, but I pray that they will be set free by the powerful message of freedom through the cross of Christ. Give them the fullness of life that we have in the resurrected Lord Jesus, by the power of his Spirit. I pray that the back of Satan would be broken in this place. No longer will he hold these people in darkness. I pray that his power will be replaced by the life-giving power of the gospel and that the Lord Jesus will be worshiped and glorified by the people of this village. In your name and for your glory I pray. Amen."

I stood up, knowing that my prayer had been an arrow hitting its mark in the heavenly realm. Not understanding what I had prayed, the monk smiled politely and motioned me back through the thick curtain. Upon exiting the monastery, I felt prompted to walk once around the building counterclockwise, praying for the presence of God to fill the place and asking for this village to be flooded by the light of the gospel.

As I exited the gate, the previously cordial monk began yelling in the angriest voice he could muster, with words obviously given to him: "Lama says, you must go!" I heard the rebuke as a confirmation of my prayer's effectiveness, as the lama had not known of my physical presence therein but had sensed the Lord's power released to break through in the spiritual realm. That evening, our team continued to pray that the power of the gospel would take root in the hearts of Kagbeni residents. Before we departed the next morning, we presented gospel booklets to the lodge owner and to several other villagers with whom we had interacted.

The days followed like dreams in living color. I never imagined that I would have the opportunity to backpack through the Himalayan Mountains. Yet here we trekked through some of the most majestic scenery that the Lord created. Still, the highlight for me was not so much the stunning beauty, but the opportunity to bring the good news of Jesus to the hearts of those who had never heard it.

Each trekking day I gave a quantity of gospel booklets to each team member, asking them to inquire of the Lord as to whom they should give them. One day we had a long descent from the elevated holy pilgrimage village of Muktinath. I took the rear as John led the team along the trail from the front. As we hiked for miles down the path that led to the lush valley below, we encountered yak trains traveling the opposite direction. The yaks carried heavy burdens of supplies for the upper villages; each train had several drivers mounted on them.

It was humorous to notice that each yak-train driver approaching our group was not watching where he was guiding the beasts but was instead head down, riveted to a brightly colored, illustrated Gospel of John booklet that someone from our team had given them down-trail. As they passed by, I whispered a prayer that the Lord would bless them with the revelation of Jesus and would water those seeds with his Holy Spirit.

As I reached the valley and passed through the village of Marpha, an unforgettable scene unfolded before me. A boy of about ten years of age stood on a tree stump in the center of the village. His hands gripped an open colorful booklet. A large group of children had gathered and were seated on the ground surrounding the lad, who was reading to them about Jesus with vivid expression. The realization struck me that the gospel was being preached by a boy who was himself hearing it for the first time. Reading aloud in Nepali, he proclaimed the good news of a God who loves them and sent his Son so that they could become his redeemed children. Through tears of joy I prayed that God's grace and blessing would grab a hold of each young heart hearing the message, especially that new young preacher.

We enjoyed a day of rest in the village of Tatopani (meaning "hot water"), named for the natural hot springs that flowed in the area. We spent most of the day soaking our weary bodies in therapeutic pools. That evening John reminded us of our big hike to Ghorepani the next morning. I had done the calculations, and we would be climbing over a vertical mile of elevation. We'd need to leave by 6:00 a.m. to get the necessary start for this long and strenuous day's journey.

While we had been relaxing in the hot waters, an elderly woman who knew John only by reputation had approached him.

"Are you the man who takes in and cares for children without any parents?" she said in Nepali.

"Yes, my wife and I now have seventeen children that we are raising as our own sons and daughters."

"I want you to take my grandchildren." She continued through tears, "I am very old. My son died and his wife also is dead. I have been left to care for this young boy and girl. I have been ill and cannot care for them any longer. When I die, I do not know what will happen to them. Perhaps they will be sold and treated as slaves. I want you to take them."

John explained that he would take the children if they arrived by first light. The woman left for her village, a half day's journey in the opposite direction, promising that she would send the boy and girl back with their uncles.

As our team prepared for our departure the next morning, the uncles arrived at the trekking lodge. They had carried the children throughout the black of night to arrive in Tatopani by 6:00 a.m. In the predawn dark, our team started up the trail with four new members: each uncle with a blanketed child slung on his back.

At first, when Kelly purposed to make friends, the children would frighten, burying their faces in their uncles' shoulders. As the day wore on, they increasingly returned her greetings with tentative smiles. The boy was five years old and his sister was two, but they resembled half that age, their bodies gaunt and stunted from malnutrition. John named the children David and Jasmine.

The next day we faced a vertical mile of muddy trail descent through lush vegetation on the other side of the mountain pass. This proved to be Kelly's most difficult day of the entire trip. On the second day of the trek, Kelly had developed toe blisters and on each heel, giant weeping abscesses. Every night I had helped her through the painful process of prying off her boots, then draining and dressing her feet. Weeks of hiking had mashed these into perpetually swelling and bleeding wounds. Though bandaged, each step of our plummeting hike shot needles up her legs. Desperate, she developed a breathing prayer to help her cope.

My own prayer throughout our trek, like Joshua, had been that the Lord would bring his kingdom to every place where I set my foot. Kelly, on the other hand, literally drenched every individual footstep in prayer. With each interval she quoted two Bible passages in tandem, end to end, like a loop reel: "I would have despaired unless I had believed that I would see the goodness of the LORD / In the land of the living. / Wait for the LORD; / Be strong and let your heart take courage" (Ps. 27:13–14 NASB). "How great is the love the Father has lavished on us, that we should be called children of God! And that is what we are!" (1 John 3:1). It was a mantra over pain-filled, fervent miles, every word matching every step.

On our third day after receiving the children, we reached a road and flagged a taxi to transport us back to Pokhara. The children began to scream as we loaded them into the passenger truck, both because they were being separated from their uncles and because they had never encountered a motorized vehicle. Arriving in Pokhara, we realized that the children had seen nothing of the modern world. We fascinated in their reactions, including their first time seeing their own faces in a mirror.

At the hotel where we overnighted, Kelly bathed the children. The dirt they shed colored the water mud-brown. She worked to scrub and clean them, as I made fast work of buying new clothing for both David and Jasmine. I returned and we wrapped the youngsters in towels and held them in front of the large bathroom mirror. David laughed as he high-fived his alternate self. Jasmine, on the other hand, simply cried and buried herself into Kelly's embrace. She eventually did look up, but with that sad girl watching back at her in the mirror, Jasmine returned to tears.

We had the privilege of being present when John's wife, Elizabeth, received her new children and saw their loving welcome from new brothers and sisters. When we departed, we knew that David and Jasmine would be happy in their new home, blessed by the love of a caring mother and father reflecting their love from Father God. It was heart wrenching to say good-bye to David and Jasmine, but in that moment, Kelly and I determined to financially support them as if they were our own.

I RECENTLY had the opportunity to speak to John through a phone call. I had a question that I had to ask him. "John, in our trek together we passed through dozens of villages. We prayed and planted gospel tracts as seeds but didn't find a single believer. I want to ask you, are there any believers or churches in any of those villages today?"

"Oh brother Marty, didn't you know?" John erupted with a contagiously joyful laugh. "There is now a fellowship of believers in every village we visited together. Surely the Lord has blessed the seeds you planted."

John and I laughed and praised God over the phone together. The Father had responded to my simple prayer about backpacking and created a priceless opportunity of prayer and harvest beyond my imagination. Epic faith has a way of opening doors to unexpected adventures. Those journeys may include breathtaking beauty or heart-striking pain, but they will always have an impact for God's kingdom when we answer his invitation with faith.

FIFTEEN

Choosing Suffering

"MARTY, I'm glad I got a hold of you. I wanted to let you know that everything is set and we leave for India in one month—"

I received the phone call from my friend Dan the day Kelly and I had returned from Nepal. He kept talking but I wasn't listening. Dan and I previously talked about going to India together, but I had not committed to anything; I had just returned from Nepal, after all.

On the way back from that trip, during a layover in Singapore, our entire team was blindsided by food poisoning after eating at a popular American fast food chain. Kelly threw up repeatedly in an airsickness bag as we zigzagged in a taxi to our guesthouse—one with bedrooms on the first floor and bathrooms far up on the third. At regular intervals throughout the night we mad-dashed for the distant restroom before exploding from both ends. After one of my later rounds, I could no longer find any strength to return to my first-floor bed, so I just laid my head on the filthy tile next to the commode, a mere sunken fixture in the floor.

With my skull pounding and my cheek pressed against the cool tile, I sensed the clear whisper of the Shepherd's voice, *Marty, would you choose this?* Though cryptic, I knew exactly what the Lord was asking: If I knew that becoming this sick was the price I would have to pay for planting gospel seeds in Nepal, would I still choose it? On that vile floor in Singapore I whispered my heartfelt response:

"You know I would. I would choose this—anything to be obedient to you. Of course I would choose it."

I finally interrupted my friend on the phone, "That's great for you, Dan. You can go to India. I'm not going anywhere. I just got back from an overseas outreach. I'm not going on another one—not in one month."

I had not prayed about my answer, nor did Kelly and I discuss it, but over the course of the next two weeks I grew increasingly miserable. I felt a nagging suspicion that maybe God intended for me to go with Dan and that my selfishness was keeping me from even considering it. One night, wide awake in bed, my mind replayed our recent Nepal adventures. I remembered the men aboard yaks studying gospel booklets and the young boy preaching to peers from his stump. Then I thought about our stopover in Singapore. My recollection of that wretched Singapore night brought me to the present realization of my great disobedience in not even prayerfully considering Dan's recent invitation. I arose the next morning with a fresh level of conviction. But before I could even explain my wrestled thoughts from the night before, Kelly confronted me across the breakfast table: "Why don't you go to India with Dan? You know you're supposed to."

Moments later I spoke with him. I apologized for my disobedience to the Lord and asked Dan if I could still accompany him to India.

"Well, I'm glad you called me today because my travel agent informed me that this is the last day to add a traveler to my itinerary. I'll need your credit card number so I can purchase your ticket."

I felt such conviction that the Lord wanted me to say yes to this trip that I gave Dan my credit card number. The charge came to $1,650, none of which I currently had. I sent out an e-mail and made some phone calls requesting financial support, but I did not receive a single response.

On the day before our departure I had received zero dollars of support for this trip. I began to struggle, questioning whether I had made the right decision, so I walked up to the base prayer chapel to spend some time with the Lord. Within moments I found myself in his presence. Despite the finances, I had a strange sense of assurance that God desired my participation on this trip, and that he would provide for my needs. He reminded me of our bathroom floor conversation in Singapore. Then quickly the scene changed: instead of being on the floor in Singapore, I was on a stage in India, preaching the gospel. This all came to me like watching a movie. Continuing in my mind's eye, I finished preaching and stepped off the stage to begin praying for individuals but was intercepted by a group of Indian police officers. (Dan and I would be going to a restricted area in India where it was illegal for foreigners to preach the gospel.) I watched as the policemen put handcuffs on me, shoved me into a car, and drove me to an Indian jail. They threw me into a cell, and when I heard the metal door snap shut, I heard the Shepherd's voice clearly ask, *Marty, would you choose this?*

This question didn't seem hypothetical in that moment or within the context of my prayer time. I struggled through fear, then thoughts of how imprisonment would affect Kelly. My focus then shifted to the suffering of my Savior. I thought of the ultimate sacrifice Jesus made on the cross so that I could be set free from sin and be reconciled to the Father. Though indescribably difficult, I could give no other response.

"Yes, Lord. I will choose this. If you want me to preach the gospel, the answer is yes. If that means that I will have to go to jail for you, the answer is yes. How could I withhold anything from you when you have given everything for me? Yes, Lord, I will choose you."

When I returned from the prayer chapel Kelly was waiting for me. I must have looked like Zechariah did to Elizabeth after returning from the temple. Kelly listened as I described everything I had just sensed. She held tightly to my hand and said, "I'm proud of you." With dripping eyes, Kelly began to pray, "Jesus, I release my husband to you and into your care. I pray that you will bring him home safely to me, but if you have another purpose for his life, I release him to be obedient to you."

The phone rang shortly after we finished praying together. I wiped my eyes and answered.

"Hey, Marty, this is Stan."

"Hi, how are you?" I replied, mostly to buy time to figure out who Stan was. As he spoke, I realized this was the businessman that Dan and I had met on the previous ministry trip when Victor the prophet prayed for us. Stan had taken Dan and me out for lunch and given each of us a generous support check for our ministries.

"So let me get to the point," Stan continued. "I heard that you are going on an outreach to India with Dan. I wanted to know: how are your finances for that trip?"

"Well, we leave tomorrow and I still need $1,650," I replied a bit sheepishly.

"Okay, that's taken care of," came Stan's abrupt reply.

"Uh, Stan—may I ask, exactly what do you mean by 'that's taken care of'?"

"It means I'll have a check in the mail to Kelly by the time you get on that plane with Dan."

That very evening Kelly and I picked Dan up from his connecting flight from Colorado Springs to Los Angeles, and we went out to a Mexican restaurant to celebrate the miraculous way God provided for this trip. The next day Dan and I left for India, and in only three days Kelly received a check from Stan for $2,000 to cover my airfare and my ground expenses. Even still, through the excitement over God's miraculous provision, there loomed a cloud of concern over the strange movie-like vision I had had about being arrested and thrown in jail.

Looking back, I now realize Dan's inexperience at arranging international travel. We ended up at a small, backward border town between Nepal and northeast India. The only hotel we could find was filthy. Rotting garbage heaped up against both walls framed a hallway path leading to our room. We pushed open the door to encounter a prison-like cell boxed in by four concrete walls, lit only by a bare bulb hanging from a wire delivering just enough electricity to flicker the area with an orange glow. Sheets on two single beds shadowed imprints of greasy brown stains, each in the shape of a person. We didn't really want to entertain thoughts about it, so we quickly turned off the orange glow and fell into bed.

The next morning Dan woke with flea bites all over his body, and I just felt itchy. We walked our way across the border into India and then began to look for a taxi to take us to Siliguri to meet Dan's contact. We rounded a street corner with our luggage in tow to find a man standing in front of a bus yelling, "Siliguri, Siliguri, fifty rupees." At just over a dollar to get to our destination, I thought things were really starting to look up for us. Dan and I climbed on board and found two seats near the back and stowed our luggage behind us. The bus lurched forward and before long we were bouncing along at a fast clip through the Indian countryside. The wind ruffled my hair as I leaned out the bus window, soaking in the landscape while my thoughts drifted back to my first visit to India.

I RECALLED my first around-the-world mission trip based out of YWAM Los Angeles eight years earlier. The outreach had started with two weeks of missions and evangelism training and the more I learned, the more I had become convinced that I wanted to be a missionary. What touched me even more deeply than the teaching was the passion for Jesus I saw in the hearts of the young missionaries around me. One young man leading worship would pound on the keys and make up lyrics as he went along. I will never forget his passionate prayer, "Lord, I want my heart to break with the things that break yours. I want to be so close to you, Jesus, that I can feel your heart beating inside of me."

By the time I left for that trip, I had two prayers ringing in my own heart: "God, where do you want me to go as a missionary?" and "Father, I want to know your heart and feel it beating inside of me."

We went to Switzerland, Germany, and France, but it was not until we reached India that the Lord answered both of my prayers. By the time our small team arrived in Bombay, many of our members were sick, and some were afraid to go outside our Salvation Army youth hostel to experience Indian culture. I went out alone, and I was unprepared for the human suffering I witnessed. I saw the sick, the crippled, and the hungry begging for food. I encountered a woman mourning over her husband's dead body. I also discovered a little fishing village by the bay where I began to fall in love with the people of India.

Something strange took place as I went back to my room at the hostel: I wept uncontrollably. Not because I felt sadness in a normal way; rather, it was as if my heart inside me was breaking. I had never experienced anything like it. The next day I convinced two of the guys from our team to go out with me. We carried children on our shoulders and played soccer with teenagers, but when I found myself alone later that day, I again met inconsolable sobbing. After the same thing took place on the third day, I began to question my sanity and called out to God through my relentless weeping.

"God, what is happening to me? Am I losing my mind? My heart is breaking inside of me and I don't understand why."

The Lord spoke to my heart with alarming clarity: "Marty, you have been praying that you might know my heart. I have revealed to you how my heart breaks for my lost children." Even as those words resonated, the Lord began to question me: "Do you think that I do not see those dying in the streets? Do you think that I do not long for those who are separated from me? Who will be my hands and who will be my feet? Who will be my mouthpiece that brings the only message that gives life?"

The tears stopped flowing but my heart pounded, sobered by the seriousness of his questioning. I felt like giving a logical response, but could I muster the courage to pray it? Finally, softly, I spoke, "Here am I, send me. I'll spend the rest of my life as a missionary in India. Just say the word."

I pondered God's response of silence to my prayer. I assumed the Lord would say yes to anyone willing to be a missionary in India. It was not until later, at our next stopover destination when my team was in Thailand, that I began to understand. During a time of worship, Jesus gave me a clear picture of going back to my church and my youth group, and he added a promise, "If you will be faithful to stay, many will be faithful to go in your place." This was a specific call to me from the Lord toward mobilizing missionaries, particularly to India and the least-reached areas of the world.

THE bus Dan and I were riding in bounced over a bump and then swayed hard, jarring my thoughts back from the memory. As we passed irrigated fields of rice and the open countryside, I spoke to Jesus, "Lord, it's amazing to be back in India where so much has happened. It was here that you showed me your heart for the lost and filled my life with purpose and direction. Lord, what do you want to teach me on this trip?"

Leaning out the window, I could see that our bus was fast approaching a village of thatched-roof, bamboo dwellings. I noticed a young man walking across the route ahead. Strangely, he did not continue crossing but halted near the center of the road and turned to face our looming vehicle. I thought, *Why doesn't that boy get out of the way?* and grew more anxious as we neared. With only a bus length between us, my eyes met his desperate, hollow gaze. A moment later he flung his body into the front of our bus.

I did not see the impact, but I heard and felt it: crushing bones and wheels lunging upward after bumping over the young man's stricken body. I looked behind and saw his lifeless frame marking the road as our bus rolled on. My heart stopped beating, and I had to remind myself to breathe. *Oh God, why did I have to witness that? Out of all the buses, why did we ride this one? Why did I have to look into that boy's eyes?* The driver afforded no time to contemplate as he sped into the next city, steered directly to the police station, turned off the engine, and walked in.

An older gentleman leaned toward Dan and me and said, "I suggest that you leave as quickly as possible. You foreigners don't want to be around when the police start asking questions." We had not considered the risk, and though still stunned, we took the man's advice, exited the bus, hailed a taxi, and disappeared.

We made it to Siliguri, found our contact, and reached our guesthouse: all a blur. I felt numb and knew I would not be all right until I could find a place to be alone with God. As I sat in bed that night in an unfamiliar place, the Lord began to bring revelation to my heart. I thought about how I had looked into that boy's eyes, and I began to see him from the Father's perspective. I wrote in my journal:

This was a child whom the Father loved deeply. And out of the billions of people on this planet, the Father mourns as if he has lost his only son. He has an infinite capacity to love. This young man was the precious work of his hands, a child for whom Christ died. He was an unfulfilled longing in the Father's heart.

He desires all to come to the knowledge of Christ. If we could only see the reality of those dying daily, slipping into their eternal destiny in the absence of the Father who loves them and created them for intimate fellowship!

The Lord used that outreach to India in amazing ways. He opened doors for us to minister in several large schools where we shared the gospel with thousands of students. Our outreach culminated in a huge gathering in the town hall. Dan ministered through his musical gifts, and I shared the message of the Father's love for each of us. We saw people profoundly moved by the gospel, and many committed to become followers of Jesus.

One of God's amazing works was what he did in my own heart. Before Dan and I had arrived in India, Jesus had asked me if I would be willing to suffer for him: to choose suffering as a cost of sharing the gospel. During this trip I had to come to grips with the idea that my life was not my own; it had been bought with the precious blood of Jesus. I did not want to hold anything back from him. I realized that epic faith chooses to follow Jesus no matter the cost.

The Lord did not require me to get arrested or thrown into jail, yet I was far from finished with fiery times of testing.

SIXTEEN

Power in Weakness

WAYNE and Dan found me crumpled in a corner at the Seoul International Airport, weeping in agony. Though mission trips to India had become a regular occurrence for me, clearly this one was going to be different.

Dan and I had been planning this trip for some time, but the schedule we planned was a bit insane. Kelly and I were speaking at a Christian high school just outside Minneapolis. We would have to catch an early flight back home to LA, where I would have a twelve-hour turnaround before meeting Dan at the airport to fly to Chennai, India via Seoul, Korea. The problem started on that first flight from Minneapolis to LA. I had acquired a cold that developed into a sinus infection. When the plane's cabin pressure changed, it felt like my head would explode. On the descent, the acute pain jabbed like an ice pick to my eardrum.

The situation raised serious consideration as to whether I should continue with the India plan. My first concern was that of permanent hearing loss, so I called Randy, an ER doctor and friend. After I explained my symptoms, Randy replied, "It might hurt like hell, but I don't think you're in danger of doing damage to your hearing." That was somewhat comforting.

My second concern was more spiritual in nature. *Lord, is this a warning from you? Are you telling me that I shouldn't go on this trip to India?* Kelly and I visited with our friends Jim and Joy and asked them to pray for us. Wise and seasoned missionaries with prophetic giftings, this elderly couple had become friends and mentors to Kelly and me throughout our years in Los Angeles. After waiting on the Lord in prayer, Joy spoke a word for me: "I sense very strongly that you are to go on this trip to India. This will be a time of testing. The Lord wants to see what you are made of. You will need to persevere, but if you pass the test you will return with a new level of spiritual authority." While her words were still sinking into my heart, she continued: "And Kelly, the Lord has given me a word for you too. By releasing your husband to go, it will have a spiritual payoff for you also."

In truth, Joy's words didn't seem any more comforting than Randy's had been, but I felt conviction in my heart to continue my India travel plans. This trip was destined as a time of testing, so Kelly and I committed in prayer that I must go.

In the remaining hours before my departure, Kelly and I had one more issue to resolve. I wanted Kelly to take a pregnancy test before I left for India. Reluctant, she didn't want to face the disappointment of another negative result. We had been wading through the depths of infertility for over four years and had endured the crushing disappointment of two miscarriages. She consented, however, to take the test, and moments later brought me into the bathroom to show me the "plus" indicator. I saw the uncertain flicker in her eyes and pulled her into my arms. "You're pregnant. We're going to have a baby! God has finally answered our prayers."

We didn't have much time to revel in the happy news as I was soon whisked out the door toward the airport. In what seemed like only moments later, I nested again in an airplane seat with India as my final destination.

The joyful excitement I felt, thinking about that positive test result, eclipsed my fear of the discomfort to come. We're going to have a child!

My pleasure was short-lived, however, replaced by rapidly increasing pain as the airplane began to climb. For the entire flight to Seoul I couldn't think; I could only endure the continual pressure I felt inside my head. Relief came when we leveled out, but when the plane began to descend, the throbbing intensified so drastically it nearly sent me through the roof. When the wheels touched ground, I could not wait to get out of that flying pressure tank.

Shortly thereafter Wayne and Dan found me hovering in the fetal position in the corner just outside the jet bridge. The prospect of one more flight was itself almost unbearable. By the time the three of us reached Chennai, I emerged limp and lifeless as a rag doll. The two practically carried me to the hotel room. The following day was a Sunday, and I became incredulous when Dan informed me that Pastor Vincent expected me to preach in the morning.

"Lord, I have nothing left to give. How can I possibly preach tomorrow?"

His response came instantly in the form of a scripture I had memorized: "My grace is sufficient for you, for my power is made perfect in weakness."

"Very well, Lord. I'll trust you to give me the strength," I murmured as I drifted off to sleep.

Pastor Vincent was a jolly little man with a heart of pure gold. Kelly and I had met him on a previous trip to Chennai and instantly fell in love with him and his family. After I preached at the first service, Pastor Vincent ushered me into his office and provided a cup of chai. "Oh, brother Marty, we are so glad you are here. You are such a blessing to me and my people. Take rest here for a moment. I will get you when it is time for the second service."

As soon as he left the room, I lay down on the concrete floor. The aching in my head had mellowed to a constant drumming, but I had lost hearing in my left ear. When I spoke, my voice echoed in my right ear as if my head was in a barrel. Strangely, God's grace was sufficient for me.

When I got up to preach again, I felt the Lord's empowerment and spoke his word boldly. Afterward I was completely drained and returned to prostrate position in Vincent's office. In those depleted moments, with my head pounding like a drum and drifting close to the edge of unconsciousness, I dreamed about the baby boy or girl Kelly carried within her on the other side of the world. Our family of two was soon to become three, and I had visions of all the things we would do together.

That first morning in India I preached for three services, then later that afternoon taught at a youth rally, followed by another church service that evening. In the midst of my brokenness, the presence of the Almighty sustained me. Vincent had prepared a similarly packed schedule for the next several days, and I kept praying that the grace of Jesus would sustain me.

On the third day Kelly called me, reaching me on Vincent's landline church number. My friend Wayne watched through the office window as I listened to Kelly's voice, and he saw my face go from pale to white. Something the size of a fist plugged my throat, and as hard as I tried, I couldn't make a sound as she began crying. When my voice finally cleared, Wayne could overhear me croaking out words: "Kelly, do you want me to come home? Just say so, and I will be on the next flight to LA."

"No, honey," her voice crackled in the receiver, "there's nothing you can do here. God has a job for you to do in India and I want you to complete it."

When I hung up the phone and stepped out of the office, Wayne was waiting for me.

"What is it?" he implored.

"She's losing the baby. Kelly's going through a miscarriage. Alone." I collapsed into Wayne's arms, sobbing.

VINCENT had planned a pioneering visit to a remote village in southern India called Pudukkottai. On a previous scouting trip to pray for the village, they discovered not a single Christian fellowship nor found one individual believer. On this trip Vincent would be bringing along my small team, his own son Charlie, and a young man he had been mentoring named Franklin. The idea was to hold an evangelistic rally, gather the new believers from that rally, and have Franklin stay behind to pastor the newly established church.

Now, in addition to my physical body being broken, my heart

was grieving as I climbed into a bus for the eighteen-hour journey to Pudukkottai. As we bumped along the narrow road I turned in my Bible to find solace. The book of Philippians had always provided words of comfort for times of testing, so I began there. When I came to the middle of chapter three, I felt that the apostle Paul was giving voice to the convictions of my own heart.

> But whatever was to my profit I now consider loss for the sake of Christ. What is more, I consider everything a loss compared to the surpassing greatness of knowing Christ Jesus my Lord, for whose sake I have lost all things.

"Jesus," I whispered, "I feel like I have lost everything to follow you. Knowing you is greater than anything I've ever given up for you."

> I consider them rubbish, that I may gain Christ and be found in him.

"I used to treasure the things of this world, but now I know that it's all garbage compared to knowing you," I continued, intermingling scripture with my supplication.

> I want to know Christ and the power of his resurrection and the fellowship of sharing in his sufferings, becoming like him in his death.

I felt the Lord's penetrating voice deep within my soul: "I know that your heart's desire is to know me and my resurrection power, but are you willing to share in my suffering? Are you willing to become like me in my death? It is through the times of entering into my sufferings that you'll find intimacy with me. I was stripped and gave all of myself when I went to the cross. It is not until you become like me in my death that I can trust you with my resurrection power."

I considered my own suffering in the dark of night as the bus rolled on: the nagging blockage and pain in my left ear, my lingering sickness, and now the hole left in my heart by a precious dream stolen by miscarriage—none of which were worth comparing to what Jesus Christ had endured for me. If my own afflictions were part of sharing in the Lord's suffering, I felt I could endure them so that he could be glorified. "Then Lord, I want to share in your suffering," I committed. "I want to be emptied of myself and become a sacrifice like you so that others might know you."

I felt Jesus' arms around me as the bus rocked me to sleep.

WE arrived early the next morning in Pudukkottai, Vincent's strategic "village," a place bustling with nearly sixty thousand people. Yet it did feel much like a village, as most of the homes displayed bamboo construction under thatched roofs.

We had much to do to prepare for the rally the following day. We advertised it as a concert at the town hall with a life-giving message. Vincent had printed out flyers, and my team walked the roads, inviting locals as final arrangements were made to secure the venue. We invited everyone from businessmen to laborers, rickshaw drivers to shop keepers. The genuine interest of many encouraged us. It did not hurt that Dan passed for an American rock star with his broad frame and long, curly brown hair. Wayne and I would tease our personal "Elvis," and Dan would reward our ribbings with a few lines from "Hound Dog" or "Return to Sender."

Despite enjoying lighter moments together, we had come for the serious work of planting a church in an oversized village that had never encountered the gospel. We prayed as we walked through crowded streets—that Jesus Christ would be worshiped and glorified here. It later became evident that the powers of darkness were not at all pleased with the light of the gospel encroaching into "their" demonic territory.

When the heat of that afternoon became unbearable, we retreated to the home where we were lodging. While taking rest, something seemed dramatically wrong with Dan. His breathing became labored. He said he felt dizzy, so he lay down on the cool stone floor. His condition continued to deteriorate by the minute. Then, quite swiftly, Dan became unresponsive. The dark shroud of impending death seemed to hover like a thick blanket around us. Dan was completely unconscious as Wayne and I frantically checked for a pulse. His faint breathing diminished, and then vanished. I desperately looked for any sign of life but found none. In that moment I had an incapacitating visualization, that of calling Dan's wife, Chris, to inform her that her husband was dead. Fear knocked the wind out of me, and I fought to suck air back into my lungs. I considered administering CPR on Dan but instinctively called for everyone to pray instead. Wayne, Charlie, and I went to our knees around Dan's motionless frame and began to cry out to God. Faith welled up inside me as I rebuked the devourer.

"You cannot take him, Satan. Dan belongs to the Most High God. We rebuke the spirit of death in Jesus' name and claim the resurrection power of the living God to restore our brother to life and perfect health. Jesus, we need you." My petition came strong and unabated, loosing my panicked incapacitation. Faith had found its footing, and within the gravity of the situation, I was expressing it. Despite the warfare and ominous sense of death, I now lacked the reluctance and self-doubt that under similar circumstances had shown my lack of faith.

As we prayed over Dan together—he would recount this to us later—he watched the scene unfold from an overhead perspective. Dan could see his frame lying on the floor, and he watched as we knelt around him to petition God and confront the enemy. At the point when we had claimed the resurrection power of Jesus, his third-person per-spective changed and he opened his eyes, encountering our joyful, tear-stained faces looking back at him.

Everything transpired so quickly that we were unsure what had actually happened. When Dan opened his eyes and sat up, I threw my arms around him and our petitions to God turned to joyful praises. "I thought we had lost you, buddy," I said, muscling a big squeeze. It was obvious that the devil did not want us in Pudukkottai sharing the gospel and was prepared to do anything to oppose us. But faith taps into the power of God to overcome the schemes of the enemy. We knew that if God was with us, then Satan was powerless to stand against us. Achieving God's plans required us to keep our focus fixed on Jesus.

The next evening we gathered early at the town hall to pray. We invited the presence of Jesus to fill that place and asked him to draw souls to himself as we gave glory to God. We were surprised to see a swarm of people assemble in the meeting hall long before the event was scheduled to begin. By the time Dan started playing his guitar, an entirely Hindu crowd had packed the venue. Dan was so gifted to draw hearts in as he sang and played. He even inspired the audience to join in on choruses proclaiming Jesus as Lord, even though most did not understand what they were singing about. I felt strong anticipation when it was my turn to bring the message.

I tried to keep it as simple as possible, describing God as the creator of the universe who formed us in his image because of his desire to have children. Vincent translated for me as I explained how all of us had broken our relationship with God by siding with Satan and believing his lies. I shared the ultimate sacrifice the Father made when he gave up his own Son to take the penalty for the punishment we deserved. I saw awe on their faces as I explained how Jesus rose victoriously from the grave and offers us forgiveness, new life, and redemption as children of God. I made it clear that to follow Jesus we must follow him alone, forsaking all other gods. Then I invited individuals to come forward if they wanted prayer to have their sins washed away and to become followers of Jesus.

I had to conceal my disappointment when absolutely no one responded—nor even moved—as if they were waiting for something else to happen. During the long silence that followed, I asked Jesus, "What do we do now?"

"Invite the sick to come forward to receive prayer in my name. My presence is here and I will heal them."

I was initially shocked by this. I had never given this kind of invitation before. In my heart I questioned, *How dare I invite listeners to come forward to be healed by Jesus?* While I was still wrestling with the Lord over this, Dan came over and whispered in my ear. "Marty, I can feel the presence of God in this place. I believe Jesus wants us to pray for the sick, and that he will heal them."

My heart was pounding, but I could argue with the Lord no more. It was clear what he wanted. "The presence of God is here in this place," I prompted. "If anyone is sick we will pray for you in the name of Jesus, and Jesus will heal you." Even as the words spilled out of my mouth, I could not believe what I was saying. But as soon as I offered the invitation, men and women began to stream forward, crowding the front. Each of us quickly paired up with a native-speaking partner and, though unrehearsed, we all began to pray in like manner. We would ask each person, "What do you want Jesus to do for you?" They would respond by describing an ailment. Then we would pray specifically for Jesus' healing to come, and finally, through our translators, we would ask if they could feel any change.

I remember a doctor who came forward and pronounced to me in perfect English, "I would like to ask Jesus to heal my right ear. I have lost all hearing. Please pray for me."

As Charlie and I placed our hands on the doctor's ear, I said a simple prayer: "Jesus, touch this man's ear. In your name, Jesus, we ask that it would be completely healed. Amen."

The man turned his head from side to side. I asked, "How is it now? Can you hear from your right ear?"

"Oh yes, I can hear perfectly now," he responded as he continued to turn his head side to side, listening from each ear in turn. "Both ears are fine now. Thank you very much for praying for me in the name of Jesus."

While still talking to this man, I heard screaming from the other side of the room. Dan and Vincent had been petitioning the Lord for a woman to regain her sight. Dan later explained that the eyes of the elderly woman were glossy white when she came forward asking for prayer. "I want to see again" was her simple request. Dan and Vincent placed their hands over the woman's eyes and prayed in the name of Jesus for healing. When they took their hands away, Dan saw something like scales fall to the ground, revealing clear, deep brown eyes. That was when she started screaming. In her native tongue she was shrieking, "I can see! I can see!"

It was nearly an hour later when we finished praying for the last person who had come forward. No one had left the hall, and every person who had requested prayer had been healed. I felt the Shepherd nudging me to repeat my invitation to become followers of Jesus. It was then that the greatest miracle of the evening occurred. Immediately a dozen hearts were opened to receive new life. Vincent gathered them into a circle to invite Jesus into their lives. It was a holy moment.

Something profound then took place as Vincent introduced this small group of new believers to Franklin. "I want you all to meet your new pastor, Franklin. He will teach you how to be followers of Jesus." Franklin made his way around the interior of the circle, looking into the eyes of each person as he greeted them and learned their names. That very evening, Jesus planted a new church that would soon grow and bring about much fruit.

I must add that one person was not healed that evening. When God's Spirit was being poured out, I asked one of our team members to pray for the loss of hearing and pain I had been experiencing in my left ear. I received nothing except a compassionate reminder that this was my time of testing, and that our trip was not yet complete.

The remainder of our time in India was extremely fruitful, but each day I endured numbing pain and total loss of hearing. As the day of our departure grew near I, began to dread the thought of getting back on a pressurized airplane. I will never forget that boarding experience. My seat was in the very back of the 747 jet, and the walk seemed a mile long as I shuffled down the aisle, dreading the agony to come. But with literally each step toward the rear of the aircraft, something began to lift from me. My head began to clear, and my ear produced popping sounds as it apparently began to open. By the time I sat down in my assigned seat, I could hear perfectly out of my left ear and was completely free of pain.

When the plane reached cruising altitude, I reached for my Bible and quietly read these words:

> But he said to me, "My grace is sufficient for you, for my power is made perfect in weakness." Therefore I will boast all the more gladly about my weaknesses, so that Christ's power may rest on me. That is why, for Christ's sake, I delight in weaknesses, in insults, in hardships, in persecutions, in difficulties. For when I am weak, then I am strong. (2 Cor. 12:9–10)

Jesus had been wholly sufficient for me in my utter weakness, and I felt both unworthy and privileged to be used by him to display his power. Reclining in my seat, I had the impression that Jesus was smiling on me. I had passed his test.

Following Jesus on epic faith journeys sometimes means taking up our cross and gladly choosing to suffer for him. At other times it means taking a trout on a dry fly on a clear summer day. I was more than ready for the latter.

SEVENTEEN

Fishing with Jesus

CRYSTAL clear water sparkled like diamonds beneath a brilliant blue Wyoming sky. As I hiked upstream in my sandals, the creek ran cold and the breeze brushed warmth against my face. Making my way to a rock bluff that disappeared into a deep blue pool, I stripped line from my reel in preparation for a perfect presentation. The grasshopper imitation hissed through the air at the end of an extra-fine tippet, alighting gently where the creek fed the upper end of the pool. I could see a flash of yellow beneath the water, making its way to the surface. I braced myself for the inevitable eruption as a German brown trout smashed my hopper in a boiling commotion. I could feel its power bending the tip of my fly rod near to the pool's surface. After a brief wrestling match, I landed the beautiful trout and admired its brilliant coloration of black and red spots. I released the fish with a breath of thanks, all the while appreciating the majestic mountains framing the stream. How was I to know that I was about to have a life-altering conversation with Jesus?

Several years had past since that fateful India trip. I had accepted an invitation to speak at a Mission Adventures program hosted for teens at a small YWAM base not far from Cody, Wyoming. Hearing that there was a blue ribbon trout stream running alongside YWAM's ranch property, I brought along my fly-fishing rod. I had been unusually restless that spring. Not that the ministry in LA wasn't going great; it was. I was carrying greater responsibility and seeing more fruitfulness than ever. Yet I could not shake an edgy feeling just below the surface. Things that I used to take in stride about Los Angeles really started bugging me.

"Oh, another smog alert. I never would have guessed it by the gravy-colored sky today." "Here I am again, bumper-to-bumper on the 405. Why is this freeway a continual parking lot?" "There's that police helicopter circling our neighborhood with its search lights beaming in our windows for the third time this week. What a shock." My ornery sarcasm became uncharacteristically common.

I figured this trip to the blue skies of Wyoming might be good for me, even if only to shake off my uneasy outlook. Bouncing along in a small twenty-passenger twin-engine prop plane, I gazed out the window, admiring the streams, lakes, and mountains below. "Lord, I really need a word from you," I mused. "I'll be giving a message for the staff tomorrow, and I pray that you would give me a word to apply both to them and to me." As I continued to stare out the window, an unexpected "word" dropped into my heart.

"Isaiah 43:18–19."

Over the previous eight years I had become accustomed to the ways of the Shepherd's voice. When a random Bible reference invaded my thoughts in answer to prayer, accompanied by a sense of his nearness, I knew it was from Jesus. I had already set my Bible on my lap for the flight, being all too familiar with the near impossibility of squeezing by fellow passengers to dig out something from a carry-on. My fingers trembled as I fumbled through the pages to find the spot.

Forget the former things; do not dwell on the past. See, I am doing a new thing! Now it springs up; do you not perceive it? I am making a way in the desert and streams in the wasteland.

What new thing? No, I don't perceive it, I thought. But somehow, deep inside, I understood that this verse held the key to that restless itch under my skin. He had my attention, and I began to ponder this word.

I didn't know what new thing God was doing. God was taking some divine initiative in my life, and whatever it was, I wanted to perceive it. I wanted to embrace it. I realized, too, that this word from God must also be for the staff I would be speaking to. When the plane's wheels hit the runway, I had a message for the next day.

I THOUGHT the teachings I delivered to the young people connected well that week. Deep stirrings in my heart added fuel to my passion, which fortified my messages. But I could not wait until Wednesday. For months I had been fasting every Wednesday, setting aside time to pray, read the Word, and sharpen my focus on Jesus. Although the discipline typically amounted to nothing spectacular, I nonetheless felt much closer to God on fasting days. The approach of this particular Wednesday felt especially like an appointment that I shouldn't miss.

When I finished teaching the morning session under a big circus tent set up for Mission Adventures, I bolted for the door. I drove a borrowed truck and followed a hand-drawn map to a particular spot where a tributary flowed into the Greybull River. Soon my Teva-clad feet were immersed in cold transparent liquid so clean that I reached down to scoop it outright for a drink. I caught and released brook trout, rainbows, and browns—pure joy running through my veins. Fly-fishing with Jesus!

After releasing a big brown that I had coaxed in the pool below the bluff, I rested on a rock beside the creek, letting the sun warm my feet. My heart felt alive. Enjoying the gentle gurgle of the stream and the breeze whispering through aspens, I looked up at the clear blue sky and posed a simple question: "Lord, is there anything you want to say to me?"

"Marty, take a look around you. What do you see?"

"I see deep blue sky and, in the distance, white-capped mountains, aspen trees, and firs arrayed in brilliant greens." Excitement emerged as I continued to describe to Jesus the beauty displayed all around me. "I see dazzling colors and sparkling reflection in the movement of the water, wildflowers blooming with bursts of blue, red, purple, and yellow."

I could have gone on to describe fragrances, sounds, and sensations, but his reply intervened as a gentle whisper in my heart, momentarily ceasing its beating. "I want to give this back to you, Marty. I want to give you the mountains."

I literally had to tell myself to take a breath. How could this be? What did this mean? I had a hundred questions, but he replied only with silence. I wanted to get the plan; he just wanted to be with me. After sitting on that rock together with Jesus for a long time, I came to the understanding that God deposited these attributes in me: my love for nature, my yearning for adventure. God created me this way. It brought joy to the Father to watch my heart come alive, enjoying the very passions he had planted within me.

We sauntered back to the truck, having shared a wonderful day of fly-fishing together—Jesus and I. My heart on fire, I began to dream again.

KELLY and I bustled along that summer with our own Mission Adventure training camps in Los Angeles, but in quieter moments my heart stole back to the words Jesus spoke to me in Wyoming: *I am doing a new thing. I want to give you the mountains.* A dream began to form in my heart that we could start a Youth With A Mission training center in the mountains of Idaho. After wrapping up another successful summer program, we took a break and headed to Pocatello to visit some close friends. Perhaps Jesus would give us more clarity about this dream while there.

By this time the Lord had answered our heart's desire for children, but not in the way we had expected. We had been praying that the Lord would bring children into our lives through whatever means he deemed best. Both our precious gifts came through the miracle of adoption. First Isaac, our fiery redhead, and then, two years later, his curly blond, blue-eyed sister, Sadie. We buckled our children into car seats in the back of our Toyota Corolla and made the long drive from LA to Idaho.

We spent the first week of September with our dear friends Jack and Katie. They had invited us to join their family at their Swan Valley cabin on the Snake River. Of course, this would involve fly-fishing. That Wednesday, everyone wanted to go for a hike, but I opted to spend some time alone. I had some questions for Jesus.

I brought my Bible and my yellow pad and eased into an Adirondack chair on the back deck overlooking the river. What a beautiful day and a beautiful backdrop, with the lawn stretching down to the river and a band of trees rising up to touch the rolling hills behind. My heart was anxious only because I had to know: Is this the dream that Jesus has for us? Is it the new thing? Does he really want to give us back the mountains?

"Lord, do you want us to move back to Idaho? Do you want us to start a YWAM base here?" I waited for his reply.

I had made it a practice to fast and pray over every speaking invitation I received. Occasionally when I had asked the Lord if I should accept an invitation to speak at a youth retreat or a conference, he would reply not with a simple yes or no, but with an actual message to share. That made it obvious for both accepting the invitation and preparing what I should say.

That's what happened this particular afternoon on the back porch of Jack and Katie's cabin. I posed my questions, expecting a yes or no answer, but the Lord gave me much more. Thoughts, ideas, dreams, and logistics all flooded in. I grabbed the yellow pad, but it was impossible to capture the torrent of ideas:

- Inquire about the camp my brother told me is for sale.
- Bless the churches in Idaho by offering a free pastor's retreat.
- Equip long-term missionaries for India.
- Be field-focused: success is measured by the lost hearing the gospel.
- Start a base in Idaho with a partner base in India.
- Function like a family with each staff member doing their part.

This went on for page after page. As my notepad filled up, I felt nudged to call my brother Rob and ask about the facility listed for sale. He had learned about an old Baptist summer camp in the mountains near Cascade, Idaho. Out of curiosity, he and a friend had toured the property and offhandedly told me about it a few years earlier. It included twelve cabins, two bath houses, a dining hall with a commercial kitchen, and a nicely sized chapel. It seemed like a good home for a missionary training center. That word about "giving me back the mountains" had been so broad, but perhaps God was narrowing it down to Idaho. I wondered aloud, "Lord, are you leading us to this camp near Cascade?"

I looked down at my volume of scribbles for a moment, then looked up and soaked in the beauty around me. Jesus had said he wanted to give me back the mountains. Now it seemed he was revealing some steps to get there.

Rob set up a realtor appointment to see the camp property the following week. We all drove up together: Rob and his wife Kim, our good friends Dave and Tina, Kelly, myself, and our two precious toddlers. We arrived to find the camp in a beautiful setting, surrounded by woodland on three sides and a meadow on the fourth. A gentle, meandering stream flowed along the northern boundary and out through the open grassland sprinkled with wildflowers. Mountainous peaks rose beyond the meadow and above the forest. A large wooden cross, painted white, stood like a sentinel watching over the camp from a peak beyond the stream.

The buildings themselves, though, were in desperate need of repair. Paint was peeling off log siding, and window shutters hung lopsided from a single hinge. Various rodents had left evidence of taking up residence. Where I saw rosy potential, Kelly, through more practical glasses, saw projects. Loads of projects.

After our tour of the camp we gathered at a half-circle fire ring and began to pray. As we did so, I had a sense that the Lord wanted this camp to become part of our heritage at YWAM Idaho. In my excitement about the Lord stirring within me, I overlooked the hint of uncertainty I sensed in Kelly's prayer.

After our time of prayer I walked out alone into the meadow, where the stream meandered through wildflowers. I became amazed by how much this place reminded me of the Wyoming stream where God had said, "I want to give you back the mountains." Now in this quiet place, alone with God, I committed my direction to the Lord: "I will pursue this property, in faith, if this is what you have for us, Lord. But I desperately do not want to miss your leading. I don't want to take a single step apart from you." I paused as I weighed the seriousness of the words I was prompted to pray. I recalled getting hit by the train, and my youthful motorcycle accident, and recognized them now as tools that God had used to break me of my pride and self-will.

Here we stood on the cusp of another major life change, and I was determined not to do it on my own. I wanted to be obedient to Jesus. "Lord, if this is not from you, I ask that you would stand in my way. I would rather have you rebuke me, even publicly humiliate me, than to allow me to go in my own direction apart from your will." I left that serene field with excitement about moving forward, tempered by the concern of not wanting to proceed alone.

When we returned to Los Angeles, it became clear to us that God was calling our season of work there to a close. My previous angst and restlessness returned as, increasingly, "the grace lifted" for living in LA. I found myself anxious for the next thing God had for us. Yet a major obstacle remained: Kelly and I were not on the same page. I wanted to get on with it, and she had caution lights flashing—even digging in her heels. We were at an impasse and knew only God could sort it out, so we made an appointment with him. Wednesday morning at nine, Kelly and I would meet with God on our old denim couch, and we would not get up until we had things settled. We even prepared questions for the engagement, listed on a fresh yellow pad, complete with space allocated for the answers God would give us:

- Is our time in LA coming to a close?
- Do you want us to move to Idaho?
- Do you want us to pioneer a new YWAM base?
- Are we to buy the camp for our YWAM vision?
- Is there anything else you want to say to us?

Kelly and I entered into the presence of God together, asking questions and patiently waiting for his response. We did not move on until we had both heard from God, mutually certain of his guidance. Kelly wisely had arranged for a sitter, because we convened on that couch for over four hours, but eventually rose up, unified in God's direction for our family. We were to move to Cascade, Idaho, purchase the camp, and start a YWAM base there. One of the words, particularly comforting for Kelly, was that this would be a place to put down roots. We would raise our children in this place and see them graduate from high school there.

With that settled, we acknowledged an important step remaining that we were reluctant to take. We needed to tell our leader, Dave, that God was moving us in a new direction. Perhaps our reluctance stemmed from the major uprooting when God called us to leave Grace Church in Pocatello. We recalled painful memories of how that had gone. We'd taken responsibility for our part of that rocky road, and did not want to repeat any mistakes. We were also aware that while no one is irreplaceable, the two of us carried the weight of responsibility and leadership for some major ministries of YWAM LA. We began to pray for Dave, that God would prepare his heart in advance for the news of our eminent departure. Dave had been our leader for eight years, and we admired his wisdom. He and his wife Debbie were counted among our closest friends, and we treasured our moments with them. We wanted to leave on the best of terms.

We scheduled a time to meet with Dave in our home. He sat down in the chair facing us. Before Kelly or I could even say a word, Dave stated abruptly, "So, do you want me to tell you what you're planning to tell me?"

I smugly thought to myself, *Why yes, Dave, give it your best shot.* I think he interpreted our side-winder smiles as an invitation to continue.

"Jesus has laid you guys on my heart over the past few weeks. As I've been praying for you, this is the sense I've gotten. First, I know that God is bringing your time with us in LA to a close. I've always known that I wouldn't have you guys forever, and I am so thankful for the years we've been able to share with you. Second, I think you have received a very clear vision from the Lord. I believe it involves pioneering something new—I just don't know where or what." He paused coyly as if for dramatic effect. "So, am I close?"

During his reveal, our expressions had changed from shocked grins to sheer astonishment. We were astounded, not to mention relieved, by the way the Lord had prepared Dave for the news we needed to share with him. The Lord had even given us confirmation through our leader that we were on the right track.

Dave carefully listened to us share the direction and plans we had discerned, and then he dispensed some characteristically wise counsel. When we were finished, he prayed for us and blessed us. "I really want to get our whole ministry behind what you are doing. Let's have the leadership team pray for you next week and when the time is right, we'll commission you from our base for the pioneering effort God is calling you to."

I was learning to practice faith for the things that God speaks. I was able to give the healing invitation in India because he spoke to me and confirmed it through Dan. Now God was teaching us to be obedient and to trust him for the new thing he was speaking to us, to leave Los Angeles and start a new base in Idaho.

Nevertheless, I was reluctant to tell my leaders about one thing Jesus had spoken to me when I filled up that yellow pad—something that sounded outlandish. God had given me a directive of epic faith proportion.

PART THREE

The Character of God

When our character is put through trial, we find out what we are really made of. When God's character is tested, it is simply his opportunity to demonstrate his glorious attributes.

EIGHTEEN

The God of the Impossible

THE Poorva Express, running from Calcutta to Kanpur, rocked back and forth as it clicked down the rails in a rhythmic lullaby. The sensation beckons one to slumber, but I was far too excited to sleep. Indian landscape drifted by in a blur, and I could hardly believe that in only a few more hours we would arrive in Kanpur. My mind drifted back to the events leading up to this scouting trip. It began with a time of prayer six years earlier when I had first heard of this city and the Savior's longing to reach it.

I had been leading our YWAM community in LA through a season of prayer and fasting—to discern which countries the Lord would have us focus on. I gave everyone at our ministry a small map of what's known as the 10/40 Window, a geographical region of the world between 10 degrees north and 40 degrees north latitude, extending from West Africa to Japan. This area constitutes the greatest need for the completion of the Great Commission. I asked our people to fast and pray, and then use a quarter to trace a circle on the map where they felt God was directing our base.

One afternoon during fasting, I found our little prayer chapel on campus empty. I knelt in prayer over the 10/40 Window map and was led to draw my own circle around northern India and Nepal. Though confident that God was putting this on my heart, I sensed something more. I persisted, "Lord, is there anything else you want to say to me?" With my eyes closed tight, I saw the following letters drift across my mind in bright red: K-A-N-P-U-R. The impression jolted me, but I had no idea what it meant. A large world map resided in the room, so I began to scan over India for clues. Like a thunderclap, the word *Kanpur* jumped at me off the wall map. I discovered that Kanpur was a major city in north central India and was, incredibly, the exact center of the small circle I had just drawn.

I knew then that Jesus wanted to direct my focus to Kanpur, India. Yet since that time my frustration mounted, as year after year I had tried to make it to this city, or send teams there for outreach, but nothing ever seemed to work. I had questioned whether God even wanted me to continue the pursuit. Once, in confused frustration, I pleaded with the Lord, "Jesus, why would you have given me such a vivid sign pointing to Kanpur if you don't want me to go there?"

Now that Kelly and I were committed to uproot and relocate to Idaho, I found myself pressing in once again. "What did you intend with Kanpur, Lord?" With clarity I perceived God say, "Now is the time for Kanpur." Then I felt like the Lord dropped a bomb on me: "Marty, I want to use you to start two mission bases at the same time, one in Idaho and the other in Kanpur."

The train continued clicking along at full speed as I contemplated the task ahead. Over the years I had been growing in my understanding of what a great, awesome, and powerful God we serve, but I had to wonder whether this present audacious goal was even possible. It will be challenging enough to pioneer a mission base in Idaho, I surmised, but to attempt to start another one literally halfway around the world, at the same time, borders on crazy. A Bible verse flashed like lightning into my mind:

Jesus looked at them and said, "With man this is impossible, but not with God; all things are possible with God." (Mark 10:27)

As if winking at me, Jesus spoke these words to my heart: "You think of these big goals as impossible, but remember, doing the impossible is my specialty."

The train screeched to a halt, announcing our arrival in Kanpur and jarring me back to my surroundings. The sign on the old British-styled railway station confirmed the destination, and we pulled our luggage off the train and onto the platform. My initial excitement was short-lived as the train chugged away and all eyes of the team of people I'd brought along turned toward me with looks that said, "So what do we do now?" I had no idea.

I had determined this to be a scouting mission. Our small team huddled on the platform to discern our next step. This rag-tag group of missionaries was an interesting mix. Phil had heard some of my out-landish India stories from the past and came along for the adventure. Wayne had accompanied me when God poured out his healing power in Pudukkottai, and now he had brought along a video camera, hoping to produce a promo for our Idaho pioneering efforts. Two women also teamed up with us: Kay-Charlotte, whom I worked with to expand Mission Adventures into an international ministry, and her friend Grace, native to India. Kay-Charlotte introduced me to Grace and her husband, Raju, only days before this. Grace and Raju were leaders in our mission who had been stirred by the Lord to start something new, but they did not yet know what it would be. When we met together, they confided in me that they believed their "something new" was connected to what the Lord had already shown me—Kanpur. Grace joined my scouting team at the last minute to determine if she and her husband were indeed being called to partner with me.

I had already found online a promising bed and breakfast called The Attic. But first we experienced the fiasco of simply getting from one place to another—making our way to the train station while being hounded by taxi drivers on the street outside. With the train ride now behind us, we settled into our rooms at The Attic, quaint accommodations that had once housed British-era military. But we had no time to rest. It was late Saturday afternoon and our departure from Kanpur was scheduled for Tuesday morning. Though we felt strongly that we were to connect with believers on Sunday, we had no specific contacts. Before boarding the train in Calcutta, a missionary had told us to find "Pastor George" in Kanpur but failed to provide contact information. Looking in the phone book proved fruitless. This was a city of four million people. We scoured the pages for churches: zero.

Venturing out from the refuge of The Attic, hoping to find a church or even a single Christian believer, we discovered why Kanpur was known as one of the dirtiest cities in India: blue smoke billowed out from noisy auto rickshaws, and brown soot poured forth from leather tanneries and factories. As for our objective, no one we asked had the foggiest idea what a Christian was, much less a church.

Finally, when Grace asked one elderly gentleman if he knew of a Christian church in the city, he began to ramble off directions in Hindi, pointing this way and that. Our hopes were high as we scurried along, struggling to keep up with Grace. When we rounded a corner, we discovered a repurposed British building that once held faithful worshipers, but now offered kettles and electronics. With obvious disappointment we returned to The Attic.

I had contacted another mission in the region that had promised to send a missionary named Pramilla to serve as a guide. I had given Pramilla our dates and guesthouse location, but there was no sign of her. That night the team shared a simple meal that had been prepared and brought to our quarters, but we sat quieter than usual as each wondered what we should do. Kay-Charlotte finally asserted, "Guys, we need to pray." She was right. India can cast a fog over missionaries, making even the most obvious answers elusive. In this moment of clarity, we joined together to seek the Lord.

"I bind the devil in Jesus' name," Kay-Charlotte began. "He has no rights in this place and no power to distract or confuse us."

"Holy Spirit, we welcome you here," Grace continued. "We completely rely on you and your guidance."

Phil added, "Jesus, we need your ideas. We can't do this on our own strength. We set aside our own ideas and declare that we need you."

"Jesus, we invite you to speak to us now," I concluded as a hush fell over the room.

After several minutes of silence our team began to pray God-directed prayers. "Jesus, I see that we are like lights coming into a very dark place," Grace declared. "The enemy does not want us here because he knows the power of the light. But we will not be thwarted. This city does not belong to him; it belongs to the Lord."

"I keep getting that Pastor George is really key," Kay-Charlotte offered. "I know we don't have any way to contact him, but I believe he is our man of peace for this city."

"Wayne, you've been quiet," I prodded. "What did you sense the Lord saying?"

"Well, I didn't want to say anything because what I got seems so outlandish," he responded. Our eyes pleaded for him to continue. "I had the impression that someone in Kanpur has been praying for the past several years that God would send a YWAM team to start a ministry in this city. And then I thought Jesus said that we would meet this person. How could that even be possible?"

We continued to seek the Lord and pray the things that he was putting on our hearts, when a knock at the door interrupted us. *Who could that be?* I wondered. *It's nearly ten o'clock at night.* We were greeted by a pleasant, yet somewhat shy, Pramilla and welcomed her into the flat. "I'm so sorry I'm late," Pramilla began apologetically. "My train was delayed. I tried to call The Attic but my cell phone was dead—"

We assured Pramilla that we were overjoyed that she was now with us. I began to explain our unsuccessful attempts to identify or connect with any Christians in the city. "Tomorrow is Sunday, and we had wanted so much to fellowship with some believers in Kanpur," I admitted.

"I do have one contact," Pramilla announced as she extracted a scrap of paper from her purse. "His name is Danny. I've never met him, but I am told that he's a missionary sent out from his church in Hong Kong. I have his number here if you'd like to call him."

I glanced at my watch indicating half past ten. It seemed late to call someone I did not know. Perhaps desperation or a nudge from the Holy Spirit overcame my reluctance.

"Hello? This is Danny," came his voice after a number of rings.

"Hi, my name is Marty," I began sheepishly, "you don't know me, but I am a YWAM missionary. We are staying at The Attic. I have brought a small scouting team here with me to see whether the Lord is calling us to start a ministry in Kanpur. We wanted to connect with some believers for worship tomorrow."

I was unprepared for his enthusiastic, accented reply: "It is great, Marty. I pick you up at 9:00 a.m. I have minivan. I take your team to my church. You will love my pastor. I will be glad for you to meet him."

"That would be wonderful. What is your pastor's name?"

"His name is C.K., but we call him Pastor George."

I almost dropped the phone. Feigning a generic response, I said, "We look forward to meeting you and Pastor George tomorrow. We'll see you at nine."

The next morning I awoke early and went to the courtyard to pray. This lovely British-style inn, overtaken by ivy, was a safe haven from the chaos beyond its walls. A beautifully manicured garden surrounded me, blooming with flowers and bordered by fruit trees. Birds sang to each other while coolness hung in the morning air. I had barely bowed my head when a proper-looking Indian man approached with a tray bearing a cup and saucer, a small milk carafe, sugar cubes in a tiny bowl, and a miniature kettle of tea. He set the tray on a bench beside the wrought iron chair on which I sat. "Your tea, sir," he announced matter-of-factly with a side-bobbing nod. He then made a slight bow and a swift departure.

I invited Jesus to my little tea party and asked if there was anything he wanted to tell me. I felt Jesus prompt me, "Be prepared, you will be giving the message this morning." I did not know how that would be possible, but I found a piece of scrap paper and began to scribble down some notes.

I had just finished sipping the last of my tea as our team assembled in the courtyard. Then Danny came whizzing up in his minivan. I approached to introduce myself.

"I am so pleased to meet you, Marty," came Danny's reply through a strong Chinese accent. Danny rambled on as our team squeezed into the minivan. "I am so happy God sent YWAM team to this city. I met YWAM peoples when I went to Singapore for mission training. When I came to Kanpur three years ago, I thought, we could use YWAM peoples to reach this city, so I have been praying for you to come here since that time." I shot a knowing glance back at Wayne, affirming that he had indeed heard from the Lord, and that Danny was the obvious, very present answer to his prayer.

We arrived and climbed the stairs to a the second floor. A packed church was already in session, resounding with much singing and clapping. The women sat on woven floor mats on one side, the men on the other. Danny directed us to some mat space toward the back, and I conveniently found myself sitting next to the pastor's son, a young man named Rajesh, who happened to speak very good English. Pastor George stood in front, holding his own when it came to loud clapping and singing in Hindi.

The clapping died down and Pastor George's prayers could be heard above the singing. After praying he began to speak to the congregation through warm and inviting eyes. Then I heard the word *America* out of the ramble of Hindi. I gave a quizzical look to Rajesh who interpreted my glance and began to translate. "My dad just said that there is a missionary team visiting us from America. After the offering, the leader will introduce his team and then preach the Word of God."

I met Pastor George for the first time when we shook hands at the front of his congregation and he humbly invited me to share the day's message. I did not even need the scribbled slip of paper from my morning garden quiet time, as God began to pour his heart out through mine. This precious group of believers was a bright and shining light in a vast sea of darkness. I began to encourage them, telling of God's faithfulness, with Rajesh at my side translating. I told them the story of how God spoke the name "KANPUR" to me before I knew what it was. "Jesus has not left you; he has not forgotten you; he has called you to be a light to this city and beyond. He is the God of the impossible and has incredible plans for each and every one of you."

After the service our team was ushered to the home of Pastor George and his wife, situated on the first floor directly beneath the worship hall. After greeting all of our team members, Pastor George began to share the story of his church.

"Eight years ago my wife and I were sent from our church in Kerala to be missionaries to Kanpur. Kerala is the state on the southwest tip of India where Saint Thomas first brought Christianity to this country in the first century. There are many churches where I come from, but here in north India, you will rarely find a person who has ever heard the name of Jesus. There were four other families who came with us to help start a church, but by the end of the first year, two families returned to Kerala. We were so discouraged. At the end of the second year we had seen only a handful of people turn to Christ. It felt like the gates of hell were standing against us. We decided to declare a week of prayer and fasting. Together we went to every major Hindu temple and every high place in the city to pray. We did spiritual warfare against the powers of darkness and proclaimed Jesus as the rightful king of this place. At the end of that week something broke in the spiritual realm, and we began to see more and more people coming to Jesus every week. It was a turning point for us, and the Lord began to establish his church in Kanpur."

Something about the timing of his story seemed peculiar. "Pastor George," I inquired, "what was the year when you had your week of prayer and fasting for this city? Do you remember the month?" My excitement grew, and I finally asked, "In which week in March did you fast and pray?"

We were astounded to hear that it was the same year, in the same month, on the same week, six years prior that so many of us were fasting and praying in Los Angeles—the same date that the Lord had spelled out "KANPUR" for me. I was in awe that this group of Indian believers had been crying out to the Lord for their city at the same time God had put that city on my heart.

Pastor George became our man of peace and opened relational doors for us in the city. Grace and her husband, Raju, decided to join us in our Idaho-India vision and began to lead the effort to start a YWAM ministry in Kanpur. Wayne helped to make a dynamic video to promote what we were doing.

It was on that very Sunday afternoon in Pastor George's living room that Jesus laid twin tracks: our base in Idaho and our base in India would begin to travel to reach an impossible destination. But Jesus was schooling me that he is the God of the impossible and that nothing is too difficult for him. I had grown much in my understanding that God-focused faith is based on his Word and his voice. Now as we began to pioneer new works, I realized it was time for an epic lesson on applying the character of God to my walk of faith.

NINETEEN

Pioneering

THE bright-eyed, elderly gentleman gripped my hand tightly, announcing, "Congratulations, young man. Your first day on the job and you've bought yourself a camp." Indeed, it felt like a historic moment, and my mind swirled with the events of the past four months that had led up to this:

- Jesus speaking to me while fly-fishing in Wyoming, "Marty, I want to give you back the mountains."
- Kelly and I meeting on the blue denim couch, wrestling to come to the unified conviction that we were to pioneer a new ministry in Idaho.
- The scouting trip to Kanpur, India, where I encountered the "God of the impossible," who asked us to start two bases at the same time.

The Lord had been walking with us through it all.

After my return to LA from the Kanpur scouting trip, I focused my efforts on launching the new base in Idaho. I worked through the official channels of our organization to receive approval to establish a new YWAM location. I began the process of applying for a nonprofit ministry status. Everything was falling into place.

Kelly and I went to Idaho to celebrate Christmas with family, where I had scheduled our first official YWAM Idaho board meeting. We met on January third to hammer out the legal matters of starting a new ministry, and the board authorized me to negotiate a purchase agreement for the camp property. The following day I drove to Boise to meet with the Camp Maranatha board of directors to discuss the purchase of their property.

I arrived at that meeting well-dressed and early, yet everyone was already present, seated formally around a large table set up in the fellowship hall of one of the camp's partner churches. After greetings and introductions, I was invited to speak. I was excited to share my vision for a new YWAM missionary training center in Idaho; they were eager to get down to business. About halfway through my well-rehearsed vision statement, a board member inquired, "Have you been authorized to negotiate a contract for the purchase of the camp?"

Trying to recover from a rather abrupt shift in the discussion, I fumbled through my messenger bag to produce meeting minutes from the day before. I slid the printed copy across the table and tried to sound confident. "Yes, I have. You will find the authorization in the form of a motion on page four of the minutes recorded from our organizational meeting." While not completely unfamiliar, I still felt like a fish out of water in these types of formal meetings; I could feel my blood pressure rising by the minute. While board members perused my document, the chairman produced a document of his own. "Here's a contract for the purchase of Camp Maranatha. As you are aware, our asking price is $250,000."

I struggled to look calm as I read through the contract, but the quiver in my hand betrayed me. *Is this really happening? I thought this was going to be a "get to know you" meeting. Lord, I need your wisdom and guidance right now.* A nearly tangible hand rested on my shoulder, bringing me inner peace and confidence.

"This contract seems in order," I announced. "I'm prepared to offer $200,000 and ask your organization to carry the loan at zero percent interest for ten years."

They seemed a bit shocked by my newfound assurance and asked if I could step out of the room so they could consider my counteroffer. At the time, I wasn't sure if we would have even qualified for a loan. I didn't know whether they would agree to carry the loan in the first place, much less at no interest.

When we reconvened, the board was prepared with a counteroffer of their own. "We are willing to accept your offer of $200,000 and will carry the loan for five years at no interest. We ask for a $15,000 down payment by March 15, with $35,000 due on August 15 at the time of closing. We will carry the balance, and you will make five annual payments of $30,000."

Hearing those numbers, the lump in my throat began to grow. It was a whole lot of money. How could Kelly and I ever come up with that kind of cash? March 15 was less than three months away. *Lord, what do you want me to do?* Before full-blown panic set in, a reassuring hand once again pressed on my shoulder and I felt his nudge to proceed.

The board chairman continued, "If this is all agreeable to you, there's still the issue of earnest money. How much are you prepared to offer today when you sign this contract?" I hadn't even thought about earnest money. I was able to sneak a look at our personal checkbook inside my messenger bag. We had a balance of $1,100. This was all that Kelly and I had for the rest of the month, for all of our living expenses. I mustered my courage, feeling out of my league. "Would $1,000 be appropriate as earnest money?"

"That would be fine," the chairman replied, while the secretary made the appropriate amendments to the contract. My nerves receded, replaced by supernatural peace as I scribbled a bold signature at the bottom of the contract. With that, everyone was on their feet expressing approval. "Congratulations, young man. Your first day on the job and you've bought yourself a camp."

This day, more than any other, finalized what God had been setting in motion: we were certifiably pioneering a new work.

Back again in Los Angeles I focused more heartily on the new base to come. With the help of friends, we created our first brochure, website, and promotional video. The work continued as an act of faith, anticipating that our vision of a new ministry would soon become a reality. Of course, there was that small issue of raising thousands of dollars!

The terms of our purchase agreement stated that our first down payment of $15,000 was due in two months, on March 15. At this point Kelly and I were the sole source, and those numbers looked impossible. We found ourselves in uncharted waters. I had never had to trust God like this before to navigate such financial seas. Rather than focusing on the size of the challenge, we would have to focus on the size of our God.

One morning at a YWAM LA staff meeting, Dave facilitated a time of prayer on behalf of Kelly and me for our new Idaho initiative. He then proceeded to take up an offering for us. About sixty-five people were present that day—all were YWAM missionaries and students living by faith. Dave instructed everyone, "Just ask Jesus if he wants you to give. Ask him for an amount and be obedient to whatever he tells you." Then he had everyone wait in silence for a few minutes to listen to the Shepherd's voice.

I will never know the stories of sacrifice made that morning, but when all the offerings and pledges were counted, it amounted to $4,000. As we approached the March date, we had the $1,000 that Kelly and I gave as earnest money and now $4,000 from this YWAM offering, but we were still $10,000 short, with one week looming.

That next Sunday a couple we didn't know very well invited us to their home after church, telling us, "We have something we would like to give you for your YWAM Idaho project." When we arrived, the size of their house impressed us, and as we entered, I noticed several gold records encased on their entry wall. Sam was an excellent musician, leading worship at our church every Sunday, but I had no idea of his accomplishments in the music industry. After a very pleasant conversation, the couple handed us a sealed envelope as they said good-bye. "We pray that this will help you get started with your new YWAM ministry in Idaho." I couldn't stand the suspense. As I drove, I slid the envelope from my shirt pocket and handed it to Kelly. "You open it, honey." Kelly ripped it open and started to scream, forcing me to pull off to the side of the road. She handed the check to me, made out to YWAM, for

$10,000. We shouted and praised God for this miracle, then with tears streaming down our faces, we thanked God for miraculously providing the first down payment on the camp.

The next hurdle became the $35,000 due August 15. While this may not seem like much money in some circles, for a missionary couple trusting God for toothpaste and postage stamps it felt like millions.

Within months, we were fully relocated to Cascade, Idaho, and preparing for our first official ministry event. This was one of the things I had listed on my yellow legal pad when Jesus gave me the ministry vision for Idaho: "Bless the churches in Idaho by offering a free pastors' retreat at the camp."

A local friend's ministry provided a church mailing list, and we prepared 500 invitations to send to Idaho pastors. The retreat was scheduled for September 13–15. I had all the letters ready to go: addressed, stuffed, and stamped, sitting in a big pile on my desk. Only one problem persisted; we did not actually own the camp. In fact, we were $20,000 short of the second down payment that was due in two weeks.

What if I invited all these pastors to come for a retreat at a camp we didn't yet own, and it all fell through? Could we even recover from such a blow? In the back of my mind I remembered my prayer a year ago in the camp's meadow, "Lord, if this is not from you, I ask that you would stand in my way. I would rather have you rebuke me—even publicly humiliate me—than to allow me to go in my own direction apart from your will." This could all be a colossal failure. Is this it, I wondered, my grand humiliation for inviting all these pastors to a camp we don't even own? If we don't get the camp, how will I explain that one?

I perceived the sound of the Father clearing his throat, halting my run down this rabbit trail of unbelief. "Marty, do you trust me or not?"

After a long pause I responded, "Yes, I trust you."

"Then mail the invitations."

Without a moment's hesitation, I gathered the letters into a cardboard box and drove to the post office. Mailing those letters put my faith into action.

Young as our children were at the time, as a family we had been praying every day together that God would provide the money to purchase the camp. That night as I prayed with our five-year-old son

Isaac, we asked the Lord for a miracle. When we finished praying, he sat upright with excited revelation.

"I know what we can do, Daddy," he proudly announced, "we can use my snowboard money to buy the camp." With that he walked across the room to retrieve his piggy bank. Since we had moved to Idaho, Isaac had his heart set on buying a snowboard and learning how to ride it as soon as the first snows fell. He had been saving his money for that goal, and in an instant he was willing to surrender it all.

"That's a great idea, son." I said through wet eyes.

The next day he and I marched into the local branch of Sterling Bank.

"We'd like to make a deposit into the YWAM Idaho checking account," I announced to a quizzical teller named Brandy standing behind the counter. Isaac had emptied the contents of his piggy bank into a ziplock bag for transport. Now he was pouring it onto the counter. Brandy helped him count it as I filled out the deposit slip.

"Okay, that's seven dollars and sixty-eight cents," Brandy said with a smile.

"Good job, little buddy," I beamed. "Thanks for helping us buy the camp."

The next day I boarded a plane headed for Seattle. Mission Adventures had invited me as their weeklong guest speaker for about seventy students preparing for a summer outreach. Ten days remained to see God provide our financing miracle, and that week I vacillated between unshakable confidence and paralyzing anxiety. In my heart I knew that God would provide, but that place between promise and fulfillment proved agonizing.

That evening I spoke about faith. "It's like the children of God when they left Egypt," I told the students. "It's always good when you have the Red Sea in front of you, mountains on both sides of you, and an opposing army quickly approaching from behind, because in that moment, faith has the opportunity to express itself. Imagine how Moses must have felt moments before that enormous sea parted. He stood on that shore with confidence because he knew God. Yet I also wonder if his palms were sweaty when he lifted up his staff to part the waters. Do you think Moses wondered whether God would really come through?"

I told the students that at this time I felt a bit like Moses right before the miracle. I shared Isaac's story—how he had given all of his snowboard money to buy the camp. I admitted that I had no idea where the rest of the $20,000 would emerge from in the next ten days but pronounced that I stood on the edge of a sea of supernatural provision. I was fully convinced that God would deliver, because I knew his character.

While hearing me speak, one of the students heard the voice of the Lord for the first time. In her heart she sensed him saying, "I want you to take up an offering to help Marty buy the camp." Yet she had remained cautious, not knowing whether the instruction truly came from God.

"Jesus, if that's really you, then have someone else bring up the idea," she prayed.

The last night of Mission Adventures typically has a service where we invite students to listen to the Lord and commit their lives to follow wherever Jesus leads them. The next morning the youth pastor told me what happened after the "commitment service." All the girls were slipping into their sleeping bags when one of them spoke up. "Hey, tonight during the service I felt like Jesus was asking us to collect an offering for what Marty is doing in Idaho."

The moment she pronounced those words, the student who had heard God's voice the first night announced, "That's right. Jesus told me the same thing on the first night but I was too afraid to say anything. Let's take the offering right now." The girls repurposed a paper bag left over from a sack lunch and started throwing in their money. Within a few minutes all the girls had contributed, so they brought it to the boys' room. The boys exhibited the same excitement over the specific directive from the Lord. They emerged from their sleeping bags, shoved money into the sack, and returned to bed.

The whole story was relayed to me in the morning, and I received a crumpled lunch sack, stuffed with cash, just prior to giving my final message. I could hardly speak, being overwhelmed by the faith and generosity of these young students.

On the flight home I lowered my tray table and counted the offering. It must have been an awkward sight—as if I had just robbed a candy store. It seemed to be coins and one-dollar bills, but as I sifted through

I found a few twenties, a fifty, and even a hundred-dollar bill, all totaling $768.34. I took a silent moment to give thanks to God, and then it hit me: God had received Isaac's gift and multiplied it by one hundred. That day the floodgates of heaven opened for us, and in the following days letters crammed our YWAM post office box. Many envelopes contained only cash: no note, no return address, only money. Hundreds of small gifts arrived that week until the total reached $20,000, and then they stopped coming.

As the week closed and the payment came due, I took a cashier's check from the bank and marched across the street to the title company to sign the closing documents. When I left through those doors, I felt like Moses moving through the Red Sea.

Three weeks later we hosted our first annual pastors' retreat at our newly acquired camp. About a dozen came. I had also mobilized intercessors to pray for each one throughout the weekend. One of the pastors explained after the weekend, "I'm not even sure why I came here. I was so discouraged that I was planning to leave the ministry. These few days enabled me to meet with God in such a personal way. I know that he is with me and has given me the courage to keep serving him through my weakness."

It's amazing what can happen when we lean on the character of God. Occasionally, God waits, knowing that fiery testing produces epic faith. He can accomplish this by testing our character. When our character is put through trial, we find out what we are really made of. When God's character is tested, it is simply his opportunity to demonstrate his glorious attributes.

TWENTY

Victory

KELLY and I busily unpacked boxes while our children explored the boundaries of their new forest-flanked yard in Cascade, Idaho. We had found our beautiful two-story log home still under construction while we were in Idaho to form our board of directors and to negotiate the purchase of the camp facility. I was awkwardly hanging my wall-sized India map in my office when I noticed a dark Buick pulling into the driveway. A man, clothed far too formally for rural Idaho, stepped out of the car as I made my way to greet him. He quickly identified me as "Mr. Marty Meyer" and then handed over an apparently important, official document. He required my signature acknowledging that I had received it, then stepped back into his sedan and drove away.

Still trying to figure out what had just gone down, I stared blankly at the envelope. I tore into it, revealing a legal notice of a construction lien filed against our house, each from a vendor that Kyle, our general contractor, had failed to pay. Standing in my gravel driveway, a sobering realization began to sink in: God would have to come through for us, or we were sunk.

WHILE finishing our season in Los Angeles and before moving to Idaho, I felt Jesus had issued a most unusual invitation: a call to fast for forty days, culminating on my fortieth birthday. The Lord had prompted me to lay a spiritual foundation for the next forty years of ministry. Along with this invitation came the idea to immerse myself in a study of the character of God. I had actually been envious of others I had known who had done forty-day fasts, but I didn't want to do it simply because it seemed super-spiritual.

Yet during our season of transition, as I felt the Lord's invitation, I was able to respond with genuine excitement. *Yes.* I counted back forty days from my birthday and set aside January 22 to March 2 in my calendar. I perceived that on the first day I should pray for the current year, the second day of my fast for the next year, and so on for the next forty days and forty years of ministry.

On the first day of my fast, Jesus gave me a word for that year—and he continued to reveal a scripture and a unique theme to apply to each of the next forty years. I dedicated time each day not only to seek him but also to the discipline of writing down what he gave to me.

Fasting for this duration proved to be a difficult challenge—there were many moments of sitting hungry with my wife and kids over meals simply to share in their company. Yet it became a precious season of growing in depth and intimacy with Jesus that I would not trade for anything. My journal became a treasure chest of wisdom and spiritual insight. I accumulated page after page from my study on the character of God, and by the end of the fast, I had a prophetic word of guidance and blessing from the Father for the next forty years of ministry.

A week after my lengthy fast had ended, we were packing the moving van for our transition to Idaho. My good and faithful friend Wayne had volunteered to drive our moving van with Kelly, myself, and the kids caravanning along in the car. Wayne and I had the van three-fourths loaded when Isaac looked up at our tight packing job, tilted his head slightly, and asked, "Daddy, are we going to take my tree house apart to fit it in the moving van?" I glanced at Wayne and could not determine whether he was going to laugh or cry. He had helped me build this palatial tree house for Isaac that was the envy of the neighborhood. I scooped Isaac up in my arms and looked him in the eyes. "I'm sorry, little buddy. We won't be able to bring the tree house with us. But, I promise, when we get to Idaho we are going to build a new tree house together." (And we did—complete with a zip line descending from it.)

Moving to Idaho would bring a fresh start and new adventure on so many levels. I was brimming with excitement and optimism fueled by the specific word Jesus had given us for the upcoming year. Whereas the word for the present year reflected the promise he gave me in Wyoming: "Behold, I am doing new things," the word for the following year—our transition year—was "Victory."

I WAS still frozen in my driveway, holding the packet of legal jargon. My heart churned with a mixture of emotion. I scanned the document demanding a $12,000 payment for construction materials that we were now being held accountable for. I cringed to think of going inside to tell Kelly. "God, how could this be happening to us? I thought you were going to protect us." Blindsided by this development, I felt so defeated. "This isn't right," I spat. "We've already paid the fair price for this house. This charge is the contractor's responsibility, not ours! How unjust that he would leave us holding the bill! Besides, isn't this supposed to be a year of victory?"

Jesus interrupted my rant, "Marty, what have I been teaching you about my character?"

I had to swallow hard before responding, "Lord, that you are always faithful. You always watch over your children. You protect those who turn to you. You are a God of justice and you hate injustice. I trust you, Lord."

"Marty, I want you not only to know me. I want to teach you to apply my character to whatever you are facing. If you truly believe that I am faithful, then call upon my faithfulness. If you believe that I am just, then appeal to my justice when you face injustice. My character is not just something you should know about me, it must be the foundation of your faith."

I stood stunned and motionless in the gravel, letting those words sink in. Before I turned toward the house, the Father dropped this final phrase into my heart: "Son, victory never comes without a battle."

I stumbled through the front door as if wounded in combat. Kelly wasted no time noticing the document. We hunkered down together and I tried to explain about the man with the Buick and my subsequent encounter with God.

"Kelly, I think that God has a lesson for us about faith. Our faith is based on the character of God." I found my train of thought and kept going, "Clearly we are facing an injustice with this lien against our house. We already paid Kyle for the house he built, but he didn't pay suppliers for materials. Now they are coming after us." Kelly listened patiently, showing obvious anger at Kyle. He had bungled plenty of things in the construction process, but we had, up to this point, no suspicion of downright dishonesty.

"We have every right to be upset with Kyle," I told her, "but I think that God is trying to teach us something crucial. We are facing an injustice, but God is a God of justice. I believe he wants us to appeal to that aspect of his character."

It took a while to simmer down enough to pray, but we finally found our hands joined, appealing to our righteous Father. "Lord, I know I need to forgive Kyle," Kelly's voice cracked as she prayed. "You know we have no way to pay this bill that has been put upon us unfairly, so all we can do is look to you."

"We are facing a huge injustice," I continued, "but we declare that you are a God of justice. We appeal to that aspect of your character and ask that you would carry out justice on our behalf. We are powerless in the battle, but you are all-powerful. Please bring a just solution to our situation."

After that time of prayer, circumstances grew worse rather than better. We received five more lien letters in the next week, totaling nearly $30,000. But our perspective had changed. We laid down our anger each time we laid each notice before the Lord. "We give this one to you too, God, and pray that you would work justice on our behalf."

It sounds simplistic, but I had never considered the power unleashed when we link our prayers with God's character. Now, with each problem we faced, we looked to the character of God first.

I told my brother Rob about the situation. He had firsthand experience dealing with Kyle, as he had overseen the completion of the house during our transition from California. His tolerance for the contractor proved even lower than Kelly's. "What you need is a good lawyer," Rob advised. "There's a guy that goes to my church; I could put you in contact with his firm."

I didn't feel right about taking Kyle to court, however, and felt God was calling us to trust him to resolve the issue. Rob sensed my reluctance. "At the very least, you should get some legal counsel," he pressed. Rob was right. We did not actually know what we were facing and needed a lawyer to inform us.

Rob put us in touch with Gavin, his attorney friend, who gave us the discounted rate of $120 per hour. Though Kelly and I kept leaning on the justice of God, we made an appointment with the attorney. We felt intimidated as we laid all of the lien notices and house-closing legal documents on Gavin's dark mahogany desk and sank into his green velvet chairs. After initial greetings, he explained that after closing on our house, all outstanding bills legally became ours. With construction liens, all the subcontractors had to do was prove that their materials were in our house, which they could easily do using invoices. "There's no fighting it," he said matter-of-factly. "All you can do is pay and then try to sue the contractor, but they usually declare bankruptcy, making it impossible to collect any money." *Oh, that's super news*, I thought as I grimaced and squeezed Kelly's hand too tightly.

Gavin spent the next twenty minutes quietly leafing through our many records. The whole time I watched the clock, acutely aware that it was costing me two dollars per minute. About the time I was thinking that we had made a terrible mistake to call this guy, he flipped another paper and said, "Huh." After an awkward pause as we hung on the edge of our seats he announced, "I think I might be able to help you."

He had noticed the words "Eagle Plan" handwritten by our realtor. After some quick research, Gavin discovered that at closing, we had unknowingly paid for an insurance rider that covered construction liens on our home. He then drafted a letter that diverted all but one of the liens to that insurance company, and we left the lawyer's office thinking that it had been the best $120 we had ever spent.

After three prayerful weeks, we received notice that our insurance rider indeed paid off $25,000 of the liens against us. Kelly and I praised God for working out justice on our behalf in a most unexpected way.

Nevertheless, we still had one remaining issue to settle. The insurance company did not pay for one of the liens, assessed at $4,000, because it had been written as a lawsuit against Kelly and me personally. We would either have to pay it or take it to court. We had been pressing into the character of God for over a month by this time, appealing not only to his justice but also to his love and faithfulness, power and mercy. We even prayed for Kyle, that God would do a deep work in his heart—that God would bring conviction, but also move him to repentance and salvation.

I finally felt led that I should personally confront Kyle about this remaining $4,000. My brother Rob called it a waste of time, saying, "You'll never get a dime out of that guy." Based on Kyle's character, Rob was right. But we were appealing to God's character.

I reached Kyle by phone one afternoon. He was fully aware of the liens filed against us for his unpaid bills. "Kyle, this may sound unusual to you, but Kelly and I want you to know that on a personal level, we have forgiven you. We don't hold ill will against you. We also want you to know that we are praying for you and we bless you." I swallowed hard before continuing. "You need to know that our insurance company just paid $25,000 in bills that rightfully belonged to you. Yet this flooring company is coming after us personally for $4,000. We both know that this bill is your responsibility, for materials you failed to pay for. I'm asking you to do the right thing. Kyle, I'm asking you to pay this bill."

There was a long silence on the phone. For a moment I thought Kyle had hung up on me. Finally, I heard his voice crack, "Okay. I'll pay it. I'm sorry. I didn't mean to cause you guys so much trouble. I give you my word. I'll pay that bill."

And he did.

ON January 1 of the following year, I turned to the page of my journal from the forty-day fast and was reminded again of the Lord's word: Victory. Yet this time I was not rejoicing but bracing for battle. I meditated on the scripture for the year:

"Where, O death, is your victory? Where, O death, is your sting?" The sting of death is sin, and the power of sin is the law. But thanks be to God! He gives us the victory through our Lord Jesus Christ. (1 Cor. 15:55–57)

Jesus won the victory for us. He gave us the victory over death, over sin, over the power of the enemy. I pondered what it cost Jesus to win the victory for us. Jesus gave his life to give us victory. He is the example. That scripture goes on to say, "Let nothing move you. . . . Your labor in the Lord is not in vain." Jesus won the victory for us, but he calls us to walk in that victory. It cost him greatly; it will cost us something too.

By the third week of January, a rash of new obstacles came over us, making the whole liens debacle look like a warm-up round. Yet the Lord had given us a new battle strategy, so we went after it.

Each time we were faced with a new challenge, we wrote it down in our prayer journal and asked, "What aspect of the character of God will we need to appeal to?" We recorded the characteristic of God next to the problem, then took it to prayer. It's amazing how small overwhelming obstacles appear when placed next to aspects of God's awesome character.

Throughout the year, this prayer journal progressed into a praise journal, as we recorded God's incredible miracles in response to our appeals to his character.

January

Battle: We owe $3,000 in ministry bills; our account balance is near zero.

Character: God is our good provider.

Answer: Three individuals each sent checks for $1,000.

February

Battle: Our well is failing. (Kyle was supposed to drill a new well when they built the house but instead hooked us up to an old failing one on the property.)

Character: God is wise; he knows the best solution for our problem (Jer. 51:15).

Answer: We found a driller who let me build log furniture in exchange for the cost of a new well.

April

Battle: A $2,000 insurance bill is due for the base.

Character: God is able to communicate; we appeal to the Holy Spirit to put this need on someone's heart.

Answer: Went to breakfast with Harry. He felt prompted to help so he wrote a check for $1,000. The Holy Spirit convicted him to take his checkbook back out and he wrote another check for $1,000 to cover the whole amount.

June

Battle: We need new counters for the kitchen at camp. The old ones are rusty and in violation of health codes.

Character: God is good (Ps. 106:1).

Answer: The father of one of our volunteer staff happened to be a metal fabricator and came to install new stainless-steel counters free of charge.

July

Battle: Our BBQ grill at the camp is broken and we have upcoming guests counting on using one.

Character: God is caring, even for the sparrows (little things) (Luke 12:6–7).

Answer: A church group donated two brand-new gas grills after their weekend at the camp.

August

Battle: Our annual $30,000 payment is due.

Character: The Lord is generous and responds to our own generosity.

Answer: Our staff gave what they had ($800) and called it the "widow's mite." God provided the rest through major gifts—one was $15,000.

September

Battle: We only have six students for our first DTS. All are uncertain if they will even come.

Character: God is faithful (Josh. 21:45).

Answer: Staff spent twenty-four hours in prayer and fasting. All six students said they would come and six new students signed up by the end of that week. God provided twelve students for our first school.

October

Battle: The transmission on our car just went out and we have extra dental bills.

Character: God is gracious (Ps. 145:8).

Answer: A friend called and asked if we had any special needs. He sent a check for $5,000 that provided for our unexpected needs.

November

Battle: God is calling us to go on an outreach to India as a family. We have to raise an extra $7,500 to do so.

Character: The Father Heart of God. He cares for those who have never heard the good news and is moved to reach them (John 3:16).

Answer: One family wants to sponsor Isaac and another family wants to sponsor Sadie. God provided for our whole family to go together.

December

Battle: Our neighbor who did excavation work for us struggles with alcohol and doesn't know Jesus.

Character: God is merciful, not willing that any should perish.

Answer: God softened his heart and he called me to ask questions about Jesus. He is even interested in our mission work.

God was teaching Kelly and me that victory never comes apart from battle. Through every struggle we reach new depths in our relationship with God. This enables us to face new challenges by specifically appealing to his character. The battle becomes an opportunity to trust in God's strength, not our own. In the words of Moses, "The Lord will fight for you; you need only to be still" (Exod. 14:14).

Our next epic battle would test not only my faith but also my ability to do the one thing that is most difficult for me—nothing.

TWENTY-ONE

Fire

LEAFING aspens and singing birds evidenced the emergence of springtime in Cascade. After long a winter, I relished spring prayer walks in the woods behind our home, and as I walked, I talked to Jesus out loud. I had been dreading the gear-up for yet another financial campaign for the camp's annual mortgage payment. For the past three years I had carried the burden of asking for money. Voicing a mild complaint to the Lord, I expressed that I had become a missionary to tell people about Jesus, not petition for funds. Resolving it to be a necessary part of my job, I asked, "Jesus, what do you want me to do about this year's annual payment?"

I heard a voice that resembled an infomercial pitchman squeezing out words for added emphasis: "It's gonna be eeeeeeeeeasy!" The fact that I recognized it as the voice of Jesus caused me to erupt with laughter. I took the bait and threw it back.

"Okay Jesus, raising $30,000 is going to be easy, you say. How will that work? Do you want me to write another letter? Make a few phone calls? What exactly do you want me to do to collect this easy money?"

"Nothing," came his abbreviated reply.

"Okay, just so I know I have this right: raising thirty grand is going to be easy and I don't have to do anything about it?" I heard nothing more but sensed a gentle peace as a breeze rustled the newly formed aspen leaves. "Huh. I guess it's going to be easy then."

When I shared this with our staff—that Jesus did not want me to initiate anything—they seemed fine with it. But as weeks wore on, it was a struggle for me to just trust and wait.

Early July arrived and we had not received any new funds for the annual payment due in less than three months. As the director of YWAM Idaho it felt negligent for me not to act, but each time I brought it back to the Lord he reminded me of his word about it being easy, and my mandate to simply rest in him.

One day a phone call interrupted my devotional time in my office at home. It was Mike, our facility manager at the camp. "Marty, I thought I should let you know that we just got a call from the US Forest Service. As a precaution, they are evacuating the whole Warm Lake area due to forest fires."

Lightning strikes had recently produced a few fires in the general area around our facility. They were not particularly threatening, but only one road runs in and out of the Warm Lake area. As such, fire management wanted to prevent fires from blocking the road and trapping people in the backwoods. They allowed no exceptions: everyone except the firefighters had to pack up and get out.

"They said it would be for only a couple of days while they get this fire under control," Mike tried to reassure me.

"I certainly hope so," I said pensively. "As you know, we have groups scheduled to use the camp the rest of the summer. It would be a real bummer to have to cancel because of evacuation." We enjoyed having church groups and youth camps at our base facility. These rental groups also provided needed revenue, revenue I counted on for the annual camp payment.

As it turned out, there was no controlling this fire. The blaze took a turn for the worse as strong summer winds fanned it. Where the fire raged hottest, giant pines exploded, sending firebrands more than a mile along the winds, starting new cluster fires. They called in more firefighters and smoke jumpers but lost ground each day, as the fire moved closer and closer to our property.

When our staff gathered to pray about this, I was impressed by God's sovereignty—that all things were under his control. If the Lord said it was going to be easy, it's going to be easy. The Lord entrusted this camp to us and he is more than able to protect it. *Father, I trust you. I believe it is all in your hands.*

The Forest Service provided a website with daily status updates—red hash marks indicating where the fire was burning and grey hash marks showing destroyed areas. One morning I sat at my desk in our log home previewing the newly refreshed map, fully aware of how close the fire was to us. By this time it was an uncontained wildfire that had been raging for over thirty days, making it impossible for any visitors to the area. We had to cancel all of our July and August groups, the loss of that revenue weighing heavily on me.

At that point a disturbing thought entered my mind: Maybe it's going to be *eeeeeasy* because the camp is going to burn down. There will be nothing left to pay for. I was immobilized by fear. Was this how the Lord was going to provide for the annual payment—by burning down the camp? The more I focused on that thought, the more anxiety afflicted me. The enemy was flooding me with doubt about God's character, and I was beginning to be swept away in its undertow.

While I was wrestling with these thoughts, my computer indicated that I had just received an e-mail—the subject: "You are an impenetrable city." It came from my friend Drevvis, whom I would consider a prophetic intercessor. (I have developed special respect for those who nurture a gift from the Lord to hear what he is saying at critical times and bring those words right back to him in the form of intercessory prayer.)

"Marty, the Lord has shown me that we need to pray for the boundaries of your camp," the e-mail read. "The enemy wants to steal what the Lord has given. We need to take a stand against the enemy and cover the very borders with prayer." The e-mail went on to cite several scriptures about boundaries, and concluded with this prayer: "Father, thank you for the protection available through prayer. As I meet with you today, I ask you to make YWAM near Warm Lake like an impenetrable city.

In the name of Jesus, my strong tower, I place boundaries of protection around Marty and his family, and the YWAM camp facility that he leads. Amen."

I immediately hit the "forward" button and distributed Drevvis's e-mail to my entire contact list. She was right: Jesus did not want the camp to burn down—the devil did. Our job was to take a stand in prayer. So I asked everyone to pray for the boundaries of our camp. I heard back from countless faithful warriors all around the world, that they were praying specifically for God's protection around our camp property.

Several days later, on Monday morning, August 13, 2007, I checked my computer for an updated fire report and map. The loading image astonished me: coming into view was a map showing the camp and its entire surrounding area shaded with grey hash marks. *Has the camp been completely destroyed?* Locked in a stare-off with the screen, and somewhat in shock, the ringing of my phone snapped me back to my home office.

"Marty, have you seen the fire report this morning?" Mark, our Forest Service liaison, asked matter-of-factly.

"I'm looking at it now," I numbly replied.

"It appears we have some good news and some bad news." He continued before I could say which I preferred first. "The bad news is that this wildfire swept through the entire area where your camp is located." He paused just long enough for my blood pressure to elevate. "The good news is that—and I have no explanation as to why—I've been told that you didn't lose a single structure on your land. We can't understand it, but it seems that the fire went around your property without burning the camp itself."

I knew why. The Lord had directed us to pray specifically for the boundaries of the camp. Thousands around the United States and the world had partnered with us in divine firefighting.

Later, when we were readmitted to our property and could assess the camp for ourselves, we heard several eyewitness accounts and came to understand and appreciate the magnitude of God's protective miracle.

The firefighters had been camped on our property. They had laid sprinkler lines, supplied by a generator-driven pump, drawing water from our little creek. The fire took a violent turn toward our camp and its intensity made it impossible to fight. The crew fled. Driving away, one firefighter looked back and caught sight of a giant fireball rolling over the camp, convincing him the place would be lost. The fires raging along both sides of the main road ultimately trapped the crew, and they called in for air support. Thankfully, a plane dumped a load of retardant chemicals along the highway, allowing the crew to escape the inferno. They could only wait it out and watch the over 100-foot-tall flames rage out of control, consuming everything in their path.

After the wildfire had decimated thousands of acres, the firefighter crew determined that it was safe to reenter the area. They also needed to address raining hotspots and assess property damage. Driving the lane back into our camp, they encountered a giant tree felled by violent winds. Not only had the tree blocked the entrance to the camp; it had also fallen directly on the main sprinkler supply line, completely choking any flow. Perhaps the Lord did not want anyone, or anything, to share the credit for his miracle.

The men used their chainsaws to slice and remove the tree from the road so they could continue into the camp, where they were shocked to find it completely intact. The fire had encroached upon the camp but was not allowed to cross any part of its circular six-acre boundary. Impossibly, some of the trees rising up from the boundary line remained green and full within the camp side but had their limbs incinerated on the opposite side. The crew quickly surveyed the property and found, to their amazement, nothing within the borders of the YWAM property had been scorched.

Nothing, that is, except cabin number seven, which sits on the farthest corner of the camp. A large spruce had caught on fire outside the boundary line and toppled into camp property alongside cabin seven. The tree had continued to sizzle with such heat that it bubbled the paint on that wall and ignited the eave's edge—now continuing to burn when firefighters arrived. They quickly doused the renegade timber and the burning corner of the structure.

Some of the Forest Service personnel later testified, "If you want to see evidence of the hand of God, just go up to that YWAM camp. It's inexplicable how it survived." I pictured a band of mighty angels with wings outstretched protecting the camp from the threatening inferno. In fact, one of the specific scriptures in Drevvis's e-mail to me had read:

> He who dwells in the shelter of the Most High will rest in the shadow of the Almighty. . . . He will cover you with his feathers, and under his wings you will find refuge. (Ps. 91:1, 4)

God had miraculously spared us from the forest fire, yet there remained the matter of the $30,000 needed for annual payment. Due to the unique circumstances of the past month, our lenders gave us extra time to get the money in.

When we finally received permission to return to the camp, it was the beginning of October. Surveying the property for the first time was like walking on holy ground. Though the smoke still lingered, the evidence of God's protective presence was physically tangible, producing reverence and awe in the core of my being.

The task of cleaning our refrigerators, however, was a different and deplorable experience. When we had evacuated, it was communicated as only precautionary—for a few days. The fire had taken out power lines, leaving the entire area without electricity for months. The food products within our refrigerators and freezers actually liquefied, confronting us with a putrid sludge.

I had received counsel that we might be eligible for an insurance settlement. Besides a thousand dollars' worth of wasted food, I was not sure what we could claim. Rob said we might be eligible for loss of revenue, which I calculated and submitted as a claim.

Bruce, the insurance adjuster, informed us we would only receive loss of revenue if there had been a structure fire. We had been evacuated as a precaution, not because of a structure fire, so we were not eligible for compensation. When Bruce and I met at the camp to review the claim, I was required to show him cabin seven since I had calculated $544.58 to fix the drooping eave and repaint the front where the paint had melted into drips.

"It appears that the corner of this building was actually on fire," Bruce noted.

"Yes, the firefighters came in and easily put it out. See, this big tree here was the culprit," I said, pointing to the charred remains lying life-lessly next to the building. I had not picked up on where he was going with his line of questioning.

"Well, it seems you had a structure fire after all. Based on the damage I'm seeing here on cabin seven, I believe I can also process your claim for loss of revenue."

Within a few weeks we received a check from our insurance company. After the deductible, it came to $7,071.38. I was amazed that God had protected the entire camp but allowed a single tree across its borders, to enflame the corner of a single cabin, to ignite eligibility for an insurance claim.

What about the remaining $22,928.62 for the payment? So many individuals were praying for us through our base's fiery ordeal and determined we needed money because of it. Unsolicited financial gifts began to roll in. When the amount reached $22,928.62, the gifts stopped coming. God provided everything we needed, exactly, to make the payment that year.

Those flames were no match for the sovereign protection of God. Epic faith often requires us to be still, watch, and pray as God does all the work. The Lord was faithful to protect us and provide the money needed for our third annual payment.

In fact, for Jesus, it was *eeeeeeeasy*!

TWENTY-TWO

Faith in Dark Days

"MARTY, I've been thinking about walking out into the woods and never turning around."

These shocking, horrifying words came straight from my wife. Kelly was not kidding, and her words emerged devoid of emotion.

"The other day I got in the car and started driving. I had no idea where I was going. I just wanted to go away. I must have been driving for hours. There are roads around here that I could just disappear on—"

This terrified me. What has happened to my wife? This is the woman whose picture permanently resides in my Bible as a bookmark to Proverbs 31. In my estimation, she is a hero of the faith, both wisdom and strength for our journey together. I had no idea she was feeling this way. To my shame, I had been too preoccupied with the success of our ministry to even notice.

Kelly didn't want to pray, nor did she want to talk about it; she just thought I should know. I started taking note of the obvious around me. Dishes piled up in the sink, laundry baskets overflowed with dirty clothes, the house a disarrayed mess, and the kids spending an inordinate amount of time zoning out in front of the TV. Those things would not typically bother me, but they very typically bothered Kelly. She enjoyed organization, productivity, and efficiency. I figured she had just not gotten around to such tasks. I did not comprehend the depth of her incapacitation at that moment—that even matching up clean white socks from a single load of laundry felt like an overwhelming obstacle. What was going on?

Somehow our sister-in-law, Kim, convinced Kelly to visit the medical clinic for evaluation. She made the appointment and only mentioned it casually as she left to see the doctor. I anxiously awaited her return; when she entered the front door she saw concern lining my face.

"Well, I aced both tests for chronic depression, the written and the physical," she announced, trying hard to be brave, but betrayed by the quiver in her voice. I rushed to Kelly, folding her into my arms. She melted. There was an odd sense of safety in verbalizing what she was going through. My solid-rock, deep-waters wife was suffering from clinical depression. As terrible as that seemed, it was better than not knowing. She explained that the doctor administered several questionnaires and then drew blood to check for medical conditions that may cause depressive symptoms. "The doctor said I was off the charts on both tests."

I had never understood or even had patience for depression up to this point. But one thing was certain: now was the time for me to be present and care for the needs of my wife. I pulled back from ministry and handled everything I could around the house. I scrubbed dishes, ran laundry, cooked and cleaned up, and took charge of kid care. I tried to encourage Kelly to sleep in, read leisurely, or take walks with me. It was excruciating for her to grapple with the realization that she was so depleted, regularly lamenting how the bottom had dropped out.

The doctor prescribed an antidepressant, and Kelly went in weekly to be monitored. We gradually gained more understanding of this illness, and as a result, I grew in my capacity to empathize. We learned that depression can be triggered by the stress of major life transitions, not just by sad events. We began to take inventory of the changes we had endured in the previous year alone:

We had lived abroad and attended an intensive school in rural Mexico for three months with two toddlers.

We uprooted and moved to Idaho after eight years of living in LA, which was a major climate change to say the least.

We began a new career, becoming the founding pioneers and directors of a new ministry.

We experienced fundraising, liens, and the threat of a lawsuit, which alone could put anyone over the top.

In addition to all these, we hosted over one hundred overnight guests in our home within the first six months of living in Cascade.

Was this the cost of pioneering, or had Kelly simply reached the limit of her personal capacity and started to shut down in self-preservation?

After about nine months it seemed that Kelly was steadily climbing out of the pit. We credited this, in part, to medication that seemed to help her. She confided that while the antidepressant kept her from bottoming out, it had also so mellowed her out that it prohibited her from experiencing heights of emotions. The lows were dispelled at the expense of joy. She was anxious to complete and conclude her prescribed regime of medication, believing that God was restoring her.

While Kelly had been clawing her way up from the bottom, I had begun to slide into it. Though nothing as dramatic as what my wife experienced, I too found myself lacking in joy, passion, and fulfillment. I felt flat. I am sure that the strain of feeling helpless contributed in part, as I watched my wife battle this foe called depression. Perhaps I had run out of steam by doubling my own efforts just trying to help out.

I had previously been so excited to study books on leadership and share insights with my team, but I had stopped reading these books altogether. Maybe my problem was something deeper—a matter of the heart.

During this time I had a strange and disturbing experience. I had been feeling abnormally tired, trying to fulfill my responsibilities, but knowing I was just going through the motions. A passionless gloom hung over my head. I didn't feel well, so I told Kelly I was going upstairs to take a nap. She tilted her head in bewilderment at my uncharacteristic announcement but said nothing.

I immediately fell into a deep sleep. I could see myself sleeping from somewhere overhead. I noticed a strange bulge under the blanket near my neck, so I reached up to pull the covering away. I was stunned to see a large, dark bat sucking blood from my neck, and I received an instant impression that it had been there for a long time—months even.

I jolted awake in a cold sweat. Though nothing was physically there, I could not stop grasping at my neck, attempting to pull off this invisible adversary. What was all that about? As much as I tried to dismiss the sinister experience, I could not deny a connection between my stale heart and whatever this bat represented.

Praying in earnest, I became convinced that this leathery thing sucking my lifeblood was related to subtle agreements I had made with the enemy. In the season that I had pulled back to care for my wife, I was the brunt of some unfair criticism. I recalled one member of my team in my office repeatedly ranting, "You are a terrible leader." As much as I considered him wrong, I found myself in the aftermath putting my leadership books on the shelf and thinking, *What's the use? I'll never be a great leader. I guess I just don't have what it takes.* Subtle agreements with the enemy.

As I continued to pray I felt God calling me to rise up and fight, to take back what the enemy was trying to steal—my joy, my vision, my heart. I recognized at once that this had been a strategy of the devil—he wanted me to lose heart.

If my adversary was so concerned about the condition of my heart, then something very powerful and precious must reside there. I pondered the implications. These had been dark days, but light was about to shine.

L A K E Cascade is an easy fifteen-minute drive from my house, but I felt impatient to show up there, as if late for a tight appointment. When I arrived at midmorning a thick fog persisted over the water, obscuring the majestic view of familiar mountains that rise just beyond the distant shore. The misty gloom mirrored my countenance, and I yearned to do something that would lift the fog smothering my heart like a damp, heavy blanket.

The brisk morning persisted as I stepped along the water's edge, beginning to pray and asking for clarity. "Jesus, what's wrong with my heart? It seems so lifeless."

I listened, but only heard lapping waves against the pebbles beneath my hiking boots. "What happened to my joy, my vision, my passion? Jesus, I don't want to admit it, not even to you, but I just don't care anymore. And that scares me the most, because that's not me. It's like I don't know who I am anymore." I floundered along the shore in silence as both literal and figurative fogs obscured all but the few paces ahead. "Jesus, are you still with me?"

A reply emerged from the vapors, in his familiar gentle whisper, "Marty, you have a good heart."

I stopped—bewildered. Looking down at my boots, I thought, How could that be? Scanning around as if I might catch a glimpse of him through the mist, I asked, "Is that even possible? Jesus, can you look at me and declare that my heart is good?"

I had grown up being taught that the heart—including my heart—was desperately wicked. Every Sunday in church I had read aloud with the congregation, "I, a poor miserable sinner, confess that I have sinned against you in thought, word, and deed." So how could Jesus possibly look at me and say that my heart was good?

I paced along the shore with an entirely new set of questions swimming in my head. "Father, you have been teaching me about your character. I know that YOU are good." Ever so slightly I perceived the fog beginning to lift from the water's surface. "You have also instructed me to represent your character to a lost world in need of hope. How can I possibly demonstrate to the world that you are good if I am desperately wicked? Perhaps that is how I once was, but now, as a new creation, I am no longer defined by my sin, but by the life of Jesus that dwells within me." Now elevated, the fog lingered overhead, providing clear sight to the opposite shore. What if it was true? What if I really did have a good heart?

I noticed just ahead of my route a rock outcropping with the sun's full light striking a section about twenty feet up. I scurried to its base and began to scramble, quickly ascending, and then turned my face toward the sunbeam. The convergence felt surreal. The fog hung all around, but I had discovered an aperture through which sunlight could drench me in full force. The sensation of warmth penetrated my skin and filled my heart. I couldn't fathom it, but I believed its truth: The Lord had given me a good heart.

The next morning I sat down at my desk early, before the sun lit up my study, knowing that I had some investigating to do. If Jesus said I have a "good heart," then certainly the Bible would indicate the same. Still, I had always been taught the contrary. I wanted to study his Word through every verse that spoke of the heart, so I began a search with my Bible software and printed the list so I could study each one.

I started with the word *heart* from both Hebrew and Greek. I discovered that the Bible references the heart as the center of one's being, including the mind, will, and emotions. In biblical language, the heart is the center of the human person and is his or her very essence. I began to apply that definition to some of the specific scriptures that I had looked up. When Jesus blessed the pure in heart, he was saying that those who are pure in the center of their being will receive the reward of seeing God. I recalled Proverbs 4:23: "Guard your heart, for it is the wellspring of life." In other words, guard the very center of your being because it springs forth life. Perhaps God really had given me a good heart, I thought, and he wanted me to protect it.

The question lingered: If the heart is the core of my being, am I essentially good or essentially bad? Is my heart pure or evil? The memory of going to church as a little boy filled my mind. I remember standing with the rest of the congregation in my stiff slacks and tight Sunday shoes reciting those words, "I confess that I, a poor miserable sinner, have sinned against God." Even then I wondered if that was really the way God looked at me: a poor miserable sinner? I thought God was my Father who loved me and I was created to be his child—but as we stood together reciting the weekly confession, a fog of guilt and shame would roll in and remind my heart that it was essentially bad.

Now as a man, I sat at my desk struggling: Is that really what the Bible teaches? I had also been taught that "the heart is deceitful above all things and desperately wicked: who can know it?" Sure enough, this verse was on my printed list: Jeremiah 17:9 (KJV). As I studied the verse, I discovered that this section of Scripture contrasts two types of men. One turns his heart away from God to trust in his own strength. That man is cursed. The other man puts his trust fully in the Lord. He is blessed. In fact, he is like a tree planted by the river and is sustained by God in times of trouble.

Only a deceitful heart would choose to turn from God and trust in one's self in the light of such obvious consequences. The Bible goes on to say, "I the LORD search the heart and examine the mind, to reward a man according to his conduct" (Jer. 17:10). If all hearts were desperately wicked, I concluded, there would be no need for God to search and examine our hearts. Furthermore, he would find none to reward.

As I contemplated these scriptures, I realized I was not really questioning the doctrine of original sin, or the depravity of man, but I was exploring the finished work of Jesus' restoration. The problem of "depravity" simply means that since the Garden of Eden and the fall of man, each one of us is in desperate need of a savior, and we can do nothing to save ourselves. I turned to Romans 5, where we find instruction about original sin—through Adam we were made sinners.

> Adam's one sin brings condemnation for everyone, but Christ's one act of righteousness brings a right relationship with God and new life for everyone. Because one person disobeyed God, many became sinners. But because one other person obeyed God, many will be made righteous. (Rom. 5:18–19 NLT)

I realized I had readily embraced the work of Adam, who by association had made me a guilty sinner, while I disproportionately undermined the work of Christ that had made me righteous. I remembered the words that God spoke over his first children in the garden. After he created Adam and Eve he looked at his handiwork and declared them "very good." Yes, Adam sinned and that was very bad. God's own masterpieces chose to introduce sin into the world. But Jesus paid the ultimate price on the cross, canceling our debt and declaring us very good again.

Skimming down my list, I found 2 Corinthians 5:17 (NLT): "Anyone who belongs to Christ has become a new person. The old life is gone; a new life has begun." The Bible describes how a complete transformation takes place when a person turns to Jesus. That reminded me of a promise God gave in Ezekiel 36:26: "I will give you a new heart and put a new spirit in you; I will remove from you your heart of stone and give you a heart of flesh." God, I realized, is well aware of the problem with our hearts. He does not intend to merely fix them. He intends to replace them.

By this time, full morning light was streaming through the window in my study, and Kelly decided to surprise me with a glass of orange juice and freshly toasted English muffins with butter and honey. She had been steadily improving and regaining her cheerful outlook.

"Looks like someone's been up early studying," she said as she nested into the chair beside my desk.

"I've been researching what the Bible says about the heart." I began. "I think I've overlooked the wholeness of the transformation of the heart: that we are no longer defined by our sin but rather identified by the righteousness of Christ."

"Okay, so what does that mean in everyday, 'simple people' language?" she prodded. It felt wonderful to see Kelly returning to her practical, dry-humored self.

"Well, I'm guessing most Christians would have no problem saying, 'I'm forgiven,' but would have a hard time saying, 'I'm good.' We accept that Jesus has transformed our life, but we may be uncomfortable accepting the implications of that transformation: that we have a new, good heart bearing the image of Christ," I declared with as much confidence as my new exploration would muster.

"And the Bible says that? That the heart of the redeemed person is good?"

My Bible was open to a passage in Matthew. "Let me read what Jesus himself said about the heart." Kelly listened as I read the following words:

A tree is identified by its fruit. If a tree is good, its fruit will be good. If a tree is bad, its fruit will be bad. You brood of snakes! How could evil men like you speak what is good and right? For whatever is in your heart determines what you say. A good person produces good things from the treasury of a good heart, and an evil person produces evil things from the treasury of an evil heart. (Matt. 12:33–35 NLT)

"So what makes a tree, or a heart, essentially good or bad?" she mused.

"Jesus is discussing the difference between being of the kingdom of God or being of the kingdom of Satan. He said that you are either with him or against him. The person who is on Jesus' side is the good tree that produces good fruit from the treasury of a good heart. The person who sides with the devil is a bad tree because his heart has not been redeemed by Jesus. He can only produce bad fruit. The person who is part of God's kingdom will naturally bear fruit consistent with the good heart that God has given him."

I paused to crunch into my delicious English muffin. "It's like your good heart, Kelly. Out of your love for me you brought a good gift. Why would it be any different in our relationship with God? When we turn to him, he transforms us and then we in turn bring good gifts from the good heart he has put in us."

"I get your point, preacher," she chuckled. "It would also explain why the enemy would want to attack our hearts. We have good things to give, but Satan would want us to believe otherwise. Maybe part of the struggle we've both been going through has been a battle for our heart."

"Exactly. The devil wants us to lose heart, to get discouraged, to be depressed, to give up. Believing that I have an evil heart, after Jesus has redeemed me, is a subtle agreement with the enemy. The adversary wants us to get our eyes off of God." Kelly nodded as I continued. "Remember how we've been learning to pray by appealing to an aspect of God's character? Well, goodness is the very essence of God's character. When Moses asked God, 'Show me your glory,' the Lord answered by revealing his goodness. I think God is encouraging us to focus on him and let his goodness flow from the new heart he has already given both of us."

"So, what we believe about ourselves will affect the way we think and the way we live," Kelly summarized. "If we believe that we are desperately wicked, poor, miserable, low-down dirty wretched sinners," she wittily embellished, "then that is what we'll have to offer. But if we embrace the truth that we are new creations, with good hearts, then we will have something good to offer the world."

I smiled at my well-matched companion. "Yes. If we're on Jesus' side, then we are essentially good and our hearts represent his goodness to those around us."

We got up and stepped outside into the fresh air. The sun was nearly overhead as it poured out light from a deep blue background. We stood together in silence, soaking in the warmth. We had been through some dark days, but today the fog had lifted and the goodness of the Lord was shining. Epic faith would emerge to take on the next challenge we would face together.

The Fear of the Lord

OUR team of eight missionaries gathered in the small living room of the house we were considering purchasing. We lacked funds to buy it, but that was nothing new. By this time, stepping out in faith had become our mode of operation—provided that it was the Lord himself calling us to take that step. Nonetheless, I felt reluctant. The last time we'd prayed about buying this place we were shot down: now I stood somewhat gun shy.

Three years previous, our pioneering team had asked the Lord whether we should purchase the little white house at 110 West Market Street in Cascade, Idaho. We desperately needed a central location to gather and to establish an office for our ministry. At the time, Kelly's and my personal home doubled as the ministry's office and headquarters. Day and night, YWAMers would let themselves in to use our home phone or Internet connection, or just to hang out. The arrangement was wearing thin our family life, particularly with two young children underfoot.

Our original team members met in our family room to inquire of the Lord. We had considered other properties in Cascade, but something kept drawing us back to this one, coupled with a sense that it would become a house of prayer for the nations. Indeed, the current owners were the pastor and wife of a vibrant church in Boise. They regarded the property as dedicated to the Lord and seemed thrilled to have YWAM purchase it for mission work. I'd been hopeful that this would become our ministry's new headquarters.

Still, when we gathered to pray, some team members heard a resounding "yes" or "go for it," while others received a "no." I remember one staff person who said "no" to buying the house quoting "throwing our pearls to swine" and suggesting the purchase would be a waste. What bothered me most was that the issue divided our team. I knew we could not move forward this way, so we let the house go. Eventually the owners pulled the property from the market and leased it to renters, whose neglect of the house showed over time. Whenever I'd drive by that little dwelling I would whisper a prayer that the Lord would release it to us, in his time, if it be his will. It was now over three years later and I unexpectedly received a call from Pastor Tri, the owner.

"Marty, we've decided to put our little white house in Cascade back on the market," his warm voice announced. "Before we do, I wanted to ask if there's any chance YWAM would still be interested in buying the property. I would offer you a fair price. If you're interested, we won't even list it."

I could hardly contain my excitement but at the same time remained cautious. Would this time be any different? Would we be unified now as a staff in hearing from God about a purchase? "That's very gracious of you, Tri," I said. "I will have to get our team together to pray over this decision."

"Of course. Why don't you take a week or two and let me know what you decide?"

I requested a door key so our team could walk through the house and pray. After perusing the property, we assembled in its tiny living room.

"I feel this place would be a great asset for our ministry," I told the team. "We could set up an office here for work and meetings."

"We could also use it to provide staff housing or hospitality for visitors," Lacy suggested.

"We could use this room for worship and times of prayer," Randy offered.

"And we wouldn't have to drive out to Marty and Kelly's house to use the Internet," Dave joked.

Laughing, I broke in to the banter. "But what's most important is what God wants. I want us to collectively ask Jesus to speak to us about buying this house. If he doesn't want us to take this step, then I don't want us to proceed. But if God is saying yes, we can trust him to provide."

We took a moment to quiet our hearts before the Lord and then prayers began to go up spontaneously, filling the room. "Lord, we want what you want. We need your direction. We take authority over the enemy: he has no right to bring confusion in Jesus' name. Father, speak to us; should we purchase this house or not?" Eventually a hush fell over the room. Then, amidst the quiet came the rustling of Bible pages and the scribbling of notes as we began to hear from the Lord.

Very few of us had participated in the house-purchasing meeting three years prior, so for most staff presently in the room this was the first time seeking the Lord about it. I invited each one to share what they sensed Jesus was saying. Lacy recorded impressions in a prayer journal.

"I got the scripture Mark 11:17, where Jesus said, 'My house will be called a house of prayer for all nations,'" Randy said.

Lacy continued, "I sense that the Lord's blessing is here and he wants us to use the house for God's kingdom."

Team members shared one by one, each speaking affirmatively that the Lord wanted us to move forward to buy the house. I did not say it at the time, but I recognized that every scripture mentioned repeated those we had received three years prior. All, that is, except for that business of throwing pearls to swine.

Dave shared last. "I don't even want to share what I heard because it doesn't make any sense." After a little prodding he conceded. "I got the scripture reference Mark 12:9, but it just reads, 'What then will the owner of the vineyard do? He will come and kill those tenants and give the vineyard to others.'"

We took time to look up the reference and realized that it was Jesus' parable of the tenants. In this story, the renters did not take care of the master's property, so in the end he had to entrust it to those who would properly care for it.

"Dave, I think this scripture totally fits our situation," I said. "And do you want to know what's really funny about it? Are you even aware of who owns this house?"

"I have no idea."

"It's the pastor of the Vineyard church in Boise. I think the Lord is telling us that the owner of the vineyard wants to entrust this house to us."

Joy spread around the room following our unified prayer time and what had been a clear leading from the Lord.

Everything fell into place after that. Pastor Tri agreed on a gracious purchase price, and our team took ownership in raising money for the down payment. I began work to secure a loan for the balance.

I approached the lending ministry that held the loan on our camp property, asking if they would also provide a loan for this facility.

"I don't think we are in a position to loan you money for the house," came the reply. "But I've talked to our board, and we are willing to forgive your final payment on the camp after you make your fourth annual payment in October." Essentially, this meant they would be giving us a debt-forgiven gift of $30,000.

"Can I have that in writing?" I responded probably too eagerly. Within ten days I received an official letter, which I found out later is what qualified us to receive a conventional loan on the new office house property.

ANOTHER event transpired simultaneously that underscored the lesson of seeking the Lord before making decisions. My friend Brad was the leader of another ministry that started just before ours. They were also in the process of buying a house for their ministry. But while our purchase moved forward, theirs was falling apart.

"Marty, I don't understand," Brad pleaded in a phone conversation. "Why does it seem like everything is going great for you guys, while apparently we are going to lose not only the house but also the down payment made by our donors?"

I didn't want to offer any easy answers but felt led to ask, "Brad, did you have the word of the Lord to buy the house?"

"What do you mean?"

"Did you seek the Lord in prayer to get his direction as to whether you should move forward with buying the house?"

"Well, we don't exactly do it that way. Our leadership team met, and we decided that it was a good business decision to purchase the house for our ministry. It just seemed right," he responded.

I didn't know what to say to Brad. I learned later that they did indeed lose the house and down payment. Even worse, shortly after that their ministry imploded and within the same year dismantled. Their team went separate ways.

Brad's question troubled me. I wondered over the difference between our two scenarios. As I contemplated, I sensed Jesus' reply: The fear of the Lord.

Before we made the move to Idaho, while serving at the YWAM base in Los Angeles, I had done an in-depth study on the fear of the Lord.

I learned that "the fear of the Lord" is biblical shorthand to describe a life fully surrendered and walking in complete obedience to God. The fear of the Lord has two attitudes: one toward sin—to hate it, and another toward God—to stand in awe of his glory. It is only natural that we should have a reverent fear of God, because he is God. In his glory he is unapproachable, in his power he is incomparable, and in his wisdom he is unfathomable.

I found over forty-five scriptures using the phrase. I studied each reference within its context and was struck by the rich promise of blessing to those who walk in the fear of the Lord.

The fear of the LORD is the beginning of wisdom, and knowledge of the Holy One is understanding. (Prov. 9:10)

Fear the LORD, you his saints, for those who fear him lack nothing. (Ps. 34:9)

He will bless those who fear the LORD—small and great alike. (Ps. 115:13)

He will be the sure foundation for your times, a rich store of salvation and wisdom and knowledge; the fear of the Lord is the key to this treasure. (Isa. 33:6)

Page after page in my journal filled up with blessings. I determined that I wanted to become a person with a life marked by the fear of the Lord, living in beautiful submission to the Savior.

One promise in particular had already become a source of hope for Kelly and me during our long struggle with infertility:

Blessed are all who fear the LORD,
    who walk in his ways.
You will eat the fruit of your labor;
    blessings and prosperity will be yours.
Your wife will be like a fruitful vine
    within your house;
your sons will be like olive shoots
    around your table.
Thus is the man blessed
    who fears the LORD. (Ps. 128:1–4)

Once, I had spent a tear-filled night of prayer after experiencing the heartbreak of another miscarriage. Blind with grief, I opened my Bible to Psalm 128 and held it above my head so the Almighty could get a closer look while I quoted it from memory. I pointed to the very place on the page and said aloud: "Look, God, it says it right here, 'Your wife will be like a fruitful vine within your house; your children will be like olive shoots around your table. Thus is the man blessed who fears the Lord.' You know I have set my heart on being a man who walks in the fear of the Lord. I trust your character and your promises. You have committed yourself in your Word. Father, I ask that you would bless us with children."

Eventually, the Lord did answer our years of fervent prayers and blessed Kelly and me with our children, albeit not in the way we would have expected. (It might require another book to tell those stories.)

In my word study, I realized that another key demonstration of the fear of the Lord is inviting him into any decision-making process. I was receiving increasing invitations to speak at retreats and conferences, so I made a commitment to fast and pray over each one. I wanted to know that if I accepted an invitation, I would go with the blessing and favor of the Lord.

Once, in my excitement, I committed to speaking for a youth retreat without praying about it. Over the next few months, whenever I tried to prepare for the event, nothing came together. Frustrated and confused, I began to complain to Jesus, asking why he would not help me with the retreat. When I finally sensed his reply, "Because I never asked you to speak for this retreat," it shocked and sobered me. I didn't know what to do. To cancel at that time would show a lack of integrity, as I had made a commitment. I began to repent.

"Jesus, please forgive me for moving in presumption. I'm so sorry for not inviting you into this decision. What do you want me to do now? I can't go there without your blessing."

I sensed his warm reply. "Go, and I will be with you. But it will be difficult."

So I did go, and it was difficult. The retreat went okay, and I felt that the Lord gave me his words to speak, but I could not help feeling in the wrong place at the wrong time. I recommitted myself to walk in the fear of the Lord, and to submit every major decision to his guidance. Earlier in my spiritual journey, I would have felt it perfectly acceptable to make decisions without seeking the Lord's direction. But God was teaching me the root of pride in thinking I could decide such matters on my own. How presumptuous to think that I could make such decisions without involving my Maker in the process. The antidote was the fear of the Lord, which became essential to my epic faith. It is a matter of maintaining singular focus on him and yielding all authority to him.

I had been learning so much that I began a list of principles in my journal.

The Fear of the Lord is:
- A life that is fully surrendered and walking in obedience to the Lord.
- Being afraid of God when our walk is sinful.

- Complete reverence of God.
- Filled with promises of the Lord's blessing.
- Hating sin.
- Demonstrated by submitting our decisions to God.
- The key to walking in righteousness.

While references to the fear of the Lord abound in the Old Testament, they are all but nonexistent in the New Testament. I began to wonder; how could New Testament writers seemingly overlook such a vital concept in our walk with God? But then I made a fascinating discovery. The fear of the Lord has a New Testament counterpart; it is called faith.

In the New Testament, when we read about Abraham being called to sacrifice his son Isaac, it is called a test of faith (Heb. 11:17). When we read the same story back in the Old Testament, the test refers to the fear of the Lord.

> Now I know that you fear God, because you have not withheld from me your son, your only son." (Gen. 22:12)

As I meditated on that story, I wrote in my journal:

> The fear of the Lord reveals our love for God. God called Abraham to take his only son that he dearly loved and offer him as a sacrifice. Here Abraham holds his child, the fulfillment of a long awaited promise in his very arms; this precious one whose name means laughter; this child who has brought such joy to this couple in the autumn of life. Now concerning this very gift-son, God seemingly asks Abraham one simple question: Do you love me more?

Abraham walked in the fear of the Lord, with a life fully surrendered. How could he withhold anything from his God? So he naturally took the next step in obedience to God. The New Testament writers called that faith, whereas in the Old Testament it was called the fear of the Lord.

I realized now that faith is the fear of the Lord and the fear of the

Lord is faith—epic faith! Ultimately both are focused on the character of God. I can walk in obedience because of who he is. I can believe him for great things because my God is great. When God said "go," Abraham said "yes" because his focus was on the One who called him. When God promised a child to Abraham and Sarah well past their child-bearing years, trust prevailed because they knew that God was able.

> Without weakening in his faith, [Abraham] faced the fact that his body was as good as dead—since he was about a hundred years old—and that Sarah's womb was also dead. Yet he did not waver through unbelief regarding the promise of God, but was strengthened in his faith and gave glory to God, being fully persuaded that God had power to do what he had promised. (Rom. 4:19–21)

In my study I noticed one more important thing: the fear of the Lord leads to friendship with God. Abraham, who walked in the fear of the Lord, is often referred to as God's friend. Some have a misconception that the fear of the Lord alienates us from God, in the sense that we feel afraid of God, but the contrary is true; the fear of the Lord is a path that leads to friendship. The fear of the Lord puts our relationship with God in proper perspective—he is God; we are not. Understanding that distinction can lead us to deeper levels of intimacy. When God calls us, and we obey, it will ultimately lead us to walk in intimate friendship with him.

I next began to study the few personalities in the Bible that had the distinction of being called friends of God: Abraham, Job, David, and John. I had a growing longing in my own heart: I want to be called a friend of God. When I voiced it as a prayer, I felt the gentle voice of Jesus reminding me of his words in John 15:14: "You are my friends if you do what I command."

Walking in obedience and the fear of the Lord leads to intimate friendship with God. This process was happening in my life.

EVALUATING the first five years of pioneering YWAM Idaho, I could look back and see evidence that the foundation of my study on the fear of the Lord lay beneath everything Kelly and I had walked out. Seeking the Lord in detail to purchase the camp, and now the office house, was an expression of the fear of the Lord. Taking what had appeared at the time to be crazy steps of faith was simply a response, in the fear of the Lord, to his voice. The fear of the Lord had taught me to focus on him when Kelly's and my personal struggles seemed dark and overwhelming.

Together our team, moving in the fear of the Lord, had purchased the little white house in Cascade. Then after making the fourth annual payment of $30,000 for the camp, the fifth and final installment was forgiven. We at last carried no debt on the camp property.

We had grown from a small pioneering team to a staff of twenty full-time missionaries. We decided to have a grand five-year celebration to commemorate pioneering YWAM Idaho and give thanks to God. During the event we marched around the camp boundary, singing songs and shouting praises, reminiscent of Nehemiah celebrating the completion of rebuilding Jerusalem's wall. We marveled at what the Lord had done in only five years' time. After all the festivities had faded, I walked out to the meadow where the Lord had first spoken to me about the camp as part of our inheritance at YWAM Idaho. It was just Jesus and me spending quiet moments beside the trickling stream.

"Well done, Marty," came his quiet voice to my heart. "We've accomplished what we set out to do."

Though the job was far from over, a sense of completion and affirmation washed over me. But what I cherished more than the accomplishment was God's friendship. We had done it together.

When we are walking in the fear of the Lord, the Father can trust us as a friend with his authority. Learning to appropriate that authority would require stepping out of my comfort zone.

TWENTY-FOUR

Appropriating His Authority

"I WANT you to pray for Sally" came the clear prompting as our family sat third row from the front in our small community church. "I want you to pray for Sally and announce that she is healed in Jesus' name."

No one wanted to say it, but from all appearances of her hollowed, ashen skin, Sally was slowly dying. As a woman in her sixties, she had, up to this point, been vibrant and vivacious. I would marvel watching her cut a fresh line of powder on the ski slopes. Sally had taught Sunday school for years, and it seemed even first and second graders had a hard time keeping up with her. She loved the Lord and had never lacked in joy or energy.

But now she sat wilted in a wheelchair in the back of the church. None of her doctors knew what was wrong with her—especially troubling with her health deteriorating quickly.

"I want you to pray for Sally." I tried to dismiss the notion at first, but it came back even stronger than before: a clear sense that I was to lead the congregation in praying for Sally's healing and announce in Jesus' name that she is healed. The thought of doing that, however, made me squirm in my seat.

Our little church was not exactly open to something that might be perceived as faith healing. Was I afraid of making God look bad if nothing happened? Or afraid of looking like some kind of fanatic myself? For a time I was frozen in indecision.

I have often been bothered to see the discrepancy between the way I prayed and the way Jesus and his disciples prayed in the Bible. Where I may plead or beg, or make a mild suggestion to the Father, the epic followers of days long ago commanded demons to flee and proclaimed healing in Jesus' name—and that's exactly what happened. *Lord, can I really do that? Can I tell Sally that she is healed in Jesus' name?* Palms sweaty, I weighed what God was calling me to do.

My heart leaped out of my chest when Kelly leaned over and whispered in my ear, "Marty, I'm getting a strong impression that you're supposed to pray for Sally's healing and anoint her with oil in front of the congregation."

Now I could not deny that Jesus was prompting me to pray for Sally. But did God have the authority to heal her, and had he really entrusted me with this authority? The answers to these questions had been settled in my heart years before.

A S A L T Y mist from the Pacific Ocean blew against my face. I had come to Ensenada, Mexico, to speak for a youth missions program, but I couldn't sleep, so I got up early and went walking along the beach. I had been wrestling with a particular question at the time: "Father, do you really entrust us, your children, with your authority still today?" I prayed out loud as the surf crashed tirelessly against the sand. "If you do trust us with your authority, why does it seem that at times our prayers make no difference at all?"

I had been feeling discouraged from unsuccessfully praying for Janice, who had been struggling with some sort of demonic oppression. Janice had recently joined staff at YWAM Los Angeles, and she had brought some heavy spiritual baggage along with her. She was moody and regularly entertained suicidal thoughts. When we prayed for her, she would become despondent, as if her body were numb and she couldn't hear us. Her eyes would remain open, but she responded as if she couldn't see us. Our prayers seemed to have no impact whatsoever. When we would stop praying, Janice would return to "normal," which in itself was disturbing.

I had been searching the Bible to determine its insight about God's authority given to us and had recorded my findings on one of my yellow legal pads. Jesus gave authority to his followers to act in his name:

> [Jesus] called his twelve disciples to him and gave them authority to drive out evil spirits and to heal every disease and sickness. (Matt. 10:1)

The Bible shows us that our lack of faith can limit Jesus' ability to work:

> He could not do any miracles there, except lay his hands on a few sick people and heal them. And he was amazed at their lack of faith. (Mark 6:5–6)

Jesus entrusted his authority to his disciples and then they went out and used it. I think he expects us to do the same:

> Calling the Twelve to him, he sent them out two by two and gave them authority over evil spirits. . . . They went out and preached that people should repent. They drove out many demons and anointed many sick people with oil and healed them. (Mark 6:7, 12–13)

Jesus has all authority and he gives it to us for the task of making disciples:

> Jesus came to them and said, "All authority in heaven and on earth has been given to me. Therefore go and make disciples of all nations." (Matt. 28:18–19)

Jesus promises authority over the nations to those who overcome:

To him who overcomes and does my will to the end, I will give
authority over the nations . . . just as I have received authority
from my Father. (Rev. 2:26–27)

We have been given power to overcome the devil:

I have given you authority to trample on snakes and scorpions
and to overcome all the power of the enemy; nothing will harm
you. (Luke 10:19)

There is a special promise given to those who are going out to spread
the gospel. Jesus said he would work with us to confirm the message we
preach:

"And these signs will accompany those who believe: In my name
they will drive out demons; they will speak in new tongues;
they will pick up snakes with their hands; and when they drink
deadly poison, it will not hurt them at all; they will place their
hands on sick people, and they will get well." . . . Then the disciples went out and preached everywhere, and the Lord worked
with them and confirmed his word by the signs that accompanied it. (Mark 16:17–18, 20))

It had been by no means an exhaustive list.

As I walked along the Ensenada beach, my mind replayed scriptures I had studied and memorized. They pounded against my mind
like the rhythm of the surf, but something did not add up. "Lord, if you
have given me authority, why can't I deal with a demon that is plaguing
Janice? I believe your power is available to me, but I have rarely experienced it."

Then I remembered something else that I had written in my journal:

By faith we appropriate the truths of God's Word. It's one thing
to believe that God loves me, yet it requires faith to allow that
truth to change me and affect my attitudes and behaviors. I can
believe that God heals, but it requires faith to receive it. Belief
says, "God can." Faith says, "God will."

I needed to exercise faith to access the authority that God has already imparted to me, I thought. I believed that it was available, but had I ever appropriated his authority by faith? I began to feel my confidence rising like the incoming tide.

"Lord, I do believe that you have entrusted your power to me," I expressed as I felt the sand beneath my bare feet. "I want to be a man of God who walks in your authority. I don't want to limit you through unbelief, but desire to exercise your authority by faith. I receive it now in Jesus' name. Amen."

Even as I prayed, I realized that a deposit had already been made into my spiritual bank account. A simple admonishment came from the Father: "I've already given you my authority—now use it."

The morning light was now painting the sky, and I felt a welling up in my chest. A righteous anger burned toward that evil spirit who had been tormenting Janice, and somehow I knew that I had authority to deal with it. As I marched across the sand, I dealt with that demon. "You had better be gone by the time I get back to LA. You no longer have the right to torment my friend Janice because I revoke your rights in Jesus' name." When I had finished praying, with no known evidence that anything had happened, I sensed that her struggle was finished. (Later, after returning home, a fellow ministry leader and I prayed for Janice and she was completely set free. It was not even a battle like before; this time we took authority over the enemy and she was instantly released from demonic thoughts and behaviors.)

Glancing at my watch, I realized it was time for me to speak at the morning youth session. By the time I made it to the lecture hall, the young people were already filing in and the worship band was playing. I delivered what I hoped was an inspiring message, and the teens piled out to depart for their day's mission work.

Just then I noticed one young man lingering behind. I could see that he wanted to talk, so I approached him.

"Hi, my name is Brian," he said, extending his hand.

"Nice to meet you, Brian."

"This mission trip has been amazing," he began and then rambled on enthusiastically. "I've never experienced anything like this before. Everyone here seems to really love Jesus. This is my first time in Mexico.

I've never been out of the United States before. I'm excited to go to the Spanish church on Wednesday night. I heard they are going to have a healing service. Maybe the Lord wants to heal me at the service Wednesday night."

While I was listening to Brian, Jesus interrupted the flow of conversation by dropping a phrase into my mind: *Maybe I want to heal him right now.* I had an immediate sense that it was the Shepherd's voice, so when Brian took a breath, I interjected.

"Brian, maybe Jesus wants to heal you right now." He stared back at me stunned.

"Uh, okay. If you really think so."

"Why not?" I smiled. As if on cue, Brian took a seat on one of the folding chairs, and I saw from the metal braces supporting both of his knees why he needed prayer. I figured I might as well jump right into it, so I knelt down and put one hand on each knee. I started with a general prayer asking the Lord to touch Brian's knees. As I continued, I heard him guiding: "I want you to rebuke the arthritis in Brian's knees." I continued praying my "generic" healing prayer while at the same time mildly arguing with that voice. *That's silly. Arthritis is something old people have. What if I pray for arthritis and he doesn't have it? I'll look foolish.* As much as I contested, the prompting only increased: "Rebuke the arthritis in Brian's knees."

Looking at the situation from the other side of my rebuttal, it occurred to me that I was willing to risk disobeying Jesus to avoid looking foolish in front of a fifteen-year-old boy. *Now that is what's silly!* I thought. So I mustered my faith and went for it: "In the name of Jesus I rebuke the arthritis in Brian's knees. I pray that fire from heaven would fall and consume any impurity in his knees and restore them to perfect health. By the Lord's authority I ask for complete healing in Jesus' name. Amen."

Brian bolted straight up out of his chair at the "Amen." He started loosening straps on his metal braces, casting each aside with the announcement, "I guess I won't be needing these anymore."

"Brian, what happened?" I asked.

"Marty, as you were praying for me I felt something like fire inside my body, moving through my knees, and I just knew that God was healing me." As if to dispel any doubt, Brian began to march around the room. "Yep, looks like they are as good as new."

I found myself sitting in that metal folding chair, watching the joy on my young friend's face as he again circled the room. Then he came near and asked, "By the way, how did you know about my arthritic condition?"

"I didn't," I admitted. "I just sensed that Jesus wanted me to pray specifically against it. I had no other knowledge that you had arthritis."

"Well, I have a very rare form of degenerative arthritis. The doctors have no treatment for it; that's why I was excited about the idea of a healing service. Apart from a miracle, I knew I'd be living in a wheelchair a few years from now. But look at me. Jesus healed me!" He turned to catch up with his group, calling over his shoulder, "Thanks for praying for me!" leaving his braces behind.

"Hey, Brian," I called out. "Take my business card. If you get any update from the doctors, send me an e-mail. Okay?"

"Sure thing." He returned, shoved the card into his pocket, and scurried off to find his friends.

(I did receive an e-mail from Brian five weeks later, after he had seen his specialist. "I told the doctors that I had been healed by Jesus," Brian stated, "but they wouldn't believe me. The doctors kept running tests on me because they couldn't find any evidence that the arthritic condition ever even existed in my body. We know the truth, don't we, that it was Jesus that healed me," he said.)

After Brian bounded out of the lecture hall, I had time to myself for the afternoon while the students were out building houses and running children's programs in surrounding villages. It was welcomed downtime, as there was so much I was still processing. Little did I know that another strange event awaited me later that night.

After I finished speaking for the evening session, the youth ran around the campus blowing off steam as I watched from the balcony. Three sixteen-year-old girls approached me and one asked, "Hey Marty, would you pray for our friend Christy?"

"I'd be happy to," I obliged as I moved a step toward Christy and looked into her eyes. I intended to ask the simple question, "How can I pray for you?" But when our eyes met, hers grew as big as saucers as terror overtook her. Christy began to recoil as if confronted by some horrific monster, and then she bolted.

Her two friends looked at one another in bewilderment, then spoke to me apologetically, "We better go look after our friend."

"If she changes her mind," I called after them, "come and get me; I'm willing to pray for Christy anytime."

So quickly abandoned, I was baffled and confused. What had Christy seen in my eyes that so frightened her? It seemed peculiar: I never thought of myself as a scary person. I returned to my room but could not shake the odd occurrence. As I prayed, an uncomfortable realization formed: that Christy herself had not been frightened, but something else had, perhaps a dark entity. I began to pray for Christy with the limited insight I had been given.

Before long a knock sounded at my door. The three girls stood in the hallway, but this time Christy spoke. "I think I'm ready for prayer now," she said timidly. "The thing is," she continued, "I've had these terrible nightmares every night for the last three and a half years. I can't remember the last time I had a decent night's sleep. I just want it to stop." She came nearly to the point of tears.

"Girls, let's just take a minute and ask Jesus how we should pray," I offered gently. We all bowed our heads and invited Jesus to come and take his rightful place with us. As soon as our hearts were quiet I sensed Jesus prompting, "Ask her if she has ever played with a Ouija board." I was familiar with this "game," which is rooted in spiritualism and supposedly used to communicate with the dead. I knew it was popular among teens and many youth thought it cool to play at parties. This time I didn't hesitate to obey the prompting.

"Christy, Jesus wants me to ask you if you've ever played with a Ouija board."

"Yes, but only one time," she admitted as she looked down at her feet.

"Ask her when she did it," came the immediate prompting.

"How long ago was that?" I asked.

"Oh, maybe three and a half years ago," came Christy's reply, followed by a stunned gaze of realization.

"Christy, I think you unwittingly left a door open to the enemy when you played that game, and he has been taunting you ever since." I had an assurance about what I should do next, and I did not want these girls to be traumatized by some strange demonic manifestation. I began gently by explaining, "Christy, I am going to speak firmly in Jesus' name to whatever it is that has been attacking you. Don't be frightened; just look into my eyes." I then addressed that evil spirit decisively, demanding that it be silent and not manifest itself in any way.

"Now, I want you to follow in a prayer of renunciation." I instructed, "Simply tell Jesus you are sorry for unknowingly exposing yourself to the enemy and then reject any hold darkness has had over you."

Christy bravely confessed her involvement and cut off any control Satan could try to exercise in her life. She stood still as I then spoke, "I address you, evil spirit, in Jesus' name. You no longer have any right to inflict Christy with fear or nightmares. God's authority has revoked your access and you are no longer welcome here. In Jesus' name, you must go and never return." Immediately came peace and finality. Then I added, "Father, as Christy sleeps deeply tonight, I ask that you would give her a beautiful dream of Jesus."

The next morning while standing in line to get my breakfast burrito, Christy nearly tackled me with a hug.

"Marty, thank you so much for praying for me. Last night was the first time in three and a half years that I got a good night's sleep and didn't wake up with nightmares. Oh, and I have to tell you, I had the most incredible dream. I was with Jesus and we were walking alongside a babbling brook through a meadow. There were wildflowers of all colors everywhere I looked. It was so peaceful. Walking with Jesus, I just knew that everything was going to be all right."

The events of that weekend in Ensenada taught me something about receiving authority from Jesus and learning how to appropriate it by faith.

SITTING within the walls now of my own local church, I knew that if I avoided praying for Sally I would be disobeying Jesus. So I slid out of my seat during the closing song and approached our pastor, seated in the front row. I relayed my prompting that we must anoint Sally with oil and pray for her healing. "Do what God has put on your heart to do," came his immediate and surprising response.

As I'd moved forward to ask Pastor's permission, Kelly had scurried back to the church kitchen and returned with a Dixie cup half full of olive oil. I invited the elders present to come forward as Kelly wheeled Sally to the front of the sanctuary. Several of us hoisted her to the platform and slid a chair beneath her.

Then I led a straightforward anointing. Kelly dipped her fingers in the oil and marked a cross on Sally's forehead as I declared, "Sally, we anoint you in the name of the Father, the Son, and the Holy Spirit." I then invited elders to ask God to heal Sally in Jesus' name. As they prayed, a fresh prompting came over me to announce Sally's healing. I felt uncomfortable making such a proclamation yet was more uncomfortable with the idea of disobeying the Spirit's prompting. So when the elders finished interceding, I announced, "Sally, in the name of the Lord Jesus Christ and by his authority, you are healed. Jesus has taken away your sickness; you are completely cured and restored in his name."

Sally did not exactly jump up and start dancing through the aisles. In fact, I felt somewhat deflated while helping her feebly walk down the steps and back into her wheelchair. But deep down I held the conviction that something had happened—that this was not the end of the story.

At church or around town I saw Sally every week or so, and each time I did, she seemed a little better. It started with her using a cane instead of the wheelchair. After that, I noticed the cane's absence and that some color had returned to her face. After several months, Sally was incredibly and completely restored, once again a model of health and vitality. She glowed.

I realized from these events that appropriating God's authority is like learning to write checks from a spiritual bank account. God is all-powerful. That is who he is. He created all that exists, and all authority belongs to him. In Scripture it is clear that the God of the universe has entrusted authority to his children in order to bring hope and healing to a hurting world. He wants us as representatives to reflect his character. We are to demonstrate his love, his mercy, and his compassion; we are also entrusted with the authority to reflect his power.

At times I still shy away from confronting the demonic, or I might chicken out at the invisible nudge to voice an epic prayer for someone in need. I am still growing. But I believe that the Word of God is clear: Jesus has empowered us with his authority to heal and to overcome the powers of darkness. I have learned to recognize the voice of God when he gives clear direction to pray for a person in need. I know the character of God and can appeal to his compassion, his power, and his Father heart for his children.

I will never have it all figured out or fully understand why some prayers produce miracles while others seem to go unanswered. But I have learned to voice epic prayers with divine authority, keeping my focus fixed on God. To live lives of epic faith we can learn to hear God's voice, stand on the promises in his Word, and pray in accordance with his character, appropriating his authority.

But how can we walk consistently in epic faith? A routine stroll through the woods would reveal a secret to living in that realm.

Standing in God's Presence

I KISSED Kelly and notified my kids, "Dad's going for a prayer walk." Within moments I strolled a trail that loops through the forest behind our house. Dew hung like diamonds on blades of grass as light filtered through spring aspen leaves and flickered across my face.

"Good morning, Jesus." I smiled as my boots paused on soft soil. "Anything you want to say to me today?"

The words had barely left my lips when "Gabriel" dropped into my heart.

What about Gabriel? I pondered.

"I am Gabriel. I stand in the presence of God," came a swift reply.

I recognized this phrase and opened the New Testament tucked in my jacket. I found the story and began to read it aloud:

In the time of Herod king of Judea there was a priest named Zechariah, who belonged to the priestly division of Abijah; his wife Elizabeth was also a descendant of Aaron. Both of them were upright in the sight of God, observing all the Lord's commands and regulations blamelessly. But they had no children, because Elizabeth was barren; and they were both well along in years.

Once when Zechariah's division was on duty and he was serving as priest before God, he was chosen by lot, according to the custom of the priesthood, to go into the temple of the Lord and burn incense. And when the time for the burning of incense came, all the assembled worshipers were praying outside.

Then an angel of the Lord appeared to him, standing at the right side of the altar of incense. When Zechariah saw him, he was startled and was gripped with fear. But the angel said to him: "Do not be afraid, Zechariah; your prayer has been heard. Your wife Elizabeth will bear you a son, and you are to give him the name John. He will be a joy and delight to you, and many will rejoice because of his birth, for he will be great in the sight of the Lord. He is never to take wine or other fermented drink, and he will be filled with the Holy Spirit even from birth. Many of the people of Israel will he bring back to the Lord their God. And he will go on before the Lord, in the spirit and power of Elijah, to turn the hearts of the fathers to their children and the disobedient to the wisdom of the righteous—to make ready a people prepared for the Lord."

Zechariah asked the angel, "How can I be sure of this? I am an old man and my wife is well along in years."

The angel answered, "I am Gabriel. I stand in the presence of God." (Luke 1:5–19)

I could relate to the plight of Zechariah and Elizabeth because of the years of travail that Kelly and I had experienced due to infertility, miscarriages, and the dry-heart sense of barrenness associated with it all. I understood the question Zechariah asked, "How can I be sure of this?" as we too had dared to hope numerous times, only to be trampled repeatedly by disappointment. But I did not immediately understand Gabriel's response.

At first I thought Gabriel was insinuating, "Do you have any idea who I am? I am Gabriel, God's favorite messenger angel." Yet as I pondered further, I realized that Gabriel was actually saying, "Do you have any idea who God is? I stand in *his presence* continually. If you were to stand in his presence, you would have no need to ask 'How can I be sure?'" Faith is being sure of what we hope for, and that faith is focused on God.

I realized I needed a shift to Gabriel's perspective. I was often overwhelmed by circumstances: I focused on the size of my problems rather than on God's immense capability. I sensed Gabriel's response inviting me to practice the presence of God. The words of Jesus came into my mind:

> I am the vine; you are the branches. If a man remains in me and I in him, he will bear much fruit; apart from me you can do nothing. (John 15:5)

The very presence of God was Gabriel's own distinguishing characteristic. He defined himself that way: as one who stands in the presence of God. What if I could say the same thing?

I perceived the Shepherd's soft voice prodding me, "Go ahead and say it."

"I am Marty—" I started, but my words trailed off. Could I really say such a thing? Was I aware of God's presence? Was I a man who walked with God? Did my relationship with God define me? I hoped so.

"Go ahead and say it."

"I am Marty. I stand in the presence of God," I recited aloud to the audience of trees.

I resumed walking now with a profound awareness of Jesus walking alongside me. "I am the temple of the Holy Spirit, who resides within me. I am an earthen vessel filled with holy presence. I can walk in the awareness that God is with me, and my life is marked by this reality. I am Marty. I stand in the presence of God."

My path looped full circle until I returned to where I had started, my house in sight. There I noticed a patch on the ground where multiple pinecones clustered. I stooped to select one and broke off a single flat seed. Several saplings only a foot or two tall emerged from this collection of cones. I looked at the seed in my hand, then to the saplings, and then slowly my eyes rose to the tops of the giants surrounding me. That enormous ponderosa came from a simple seed, like this one here in my hand. The stark contrast was mind-boggling. How could that mighty giant emerge from something so small and seemingly insignificant?

As I stood among the smattering of pinecones, among saplings reaching up to my waist, and yet surrounded by living towers piercing the sky, Jesus planted in me an idea about "dream seeds."

"I've planted dream seeds in the hearts of all of my children," he said. "To grow, they require faith and the soil of my presence."

I remained motionless in that spot, trying to absorb the Lord's instruction. What are the dream seeds that the Lord has sown in my heart? How have I practiced faith to nourish their growth? How can I remain in his presence so they will mature?

Pondering these questions, a revelation humbled me: At this point in my life, some of my dream seeds had already risen into giant trees; others were like the saplings at my waist; and still others remained dormant like the one in my hand. More dreams were yet to germinate. It reminded me of parables Jesus told:

> He told them another parable: "The kingdom of heaven is like a mustard seed, which a man took and planted in his field. Though it is the smallest of all your seeds, yet when it grows, it is the largest of garden plants and becomes a tree, so that the birds of the air come and perch in its branches." (Matt. 13:31–32)

> He replied, "Because you have so little faith. I tell you the truth, if you have faith as small as a mustard seed, you can say to this mountain, 'Move from here to there' and it will move. Nothing will be impossible for you." (Matt. 17:20–21)

The size of our faith is of no consequence. The focus of our faith is what matters—and the focus is God. More specifically, our faith is rooted in the character of God. God was revealing his presence to me—his omnipresence, his presence everywhere at once. One of Jesus' names is Emmanuel, "God with us." Jesus came to show us that God is not distant—not way off in heaven somewhere—but walking right with us. He is involved in our lives.

If I could remain aware of this truth of his character, then I could be a branch connected to the vine, continually bearing much fruit. My dreams could be like tiny seeds nourished to become mighty trees. Rooted in the presence of God, my prayers could move mountains. I could be like Gabriel, defined by God's nearness. The presence of God makes the difference.

I began to think of men and women of epic faith. I rushed home, sat down at my desk, and grabbed a fresh notepad. I recorded biblical characters whose lives were transformed by the presence of the living God:

Moses: An insecure shepherd doubting his destiny until he met the Great I AM in the burning bush. He was transformed into a powerful man of God.

Peter: An ordinary fisherman, full of himself until he met the Fisher of men. After he witnessed a miraculous catch he proclaimed, "Depart from me Lord, for I am a sinful man." Peter was transformed into a rock who stood fearless, proclaiming Jesus as Savior and Lord.

Mary Magdalene: A sinful, demon-possessed woman until she met the merciful Savior. She was transformed into a woman of God whose love and devotion for Jesus was unparalleled.

Saul: A self-righteous Christian-killer who was blinded by the glory of the risen Christ! He was transformed into the humble apostle who suffered for the Lord in order to make the Lord's name known among the Gentiles.

What did all of these people have in common? They were never the same after meeting the God who transforms. They were forever changed by the presence of God in their lives.

Over the course of the next several days, I found myself more aware of God's presence. Not in some vague theological sense, but rather the kind of awareness that says, "Good morning, Jesus," when you first wake up. My appetite for God's presence was growing, and I found myself gravitating toward characters from Scripture that could teach me more about being in his presence. The following morning I read from the book of Exodus:

> Now Moses used to take a tent and pitch it outside the camp some distance away, calling it the "tent of meeting." Anyone inquiring of the LORD would go to the tent of meeting outside the camp. And whenever Moses went out to the tent, all the people rose and stood at the entrances to their tents, watching Moses until he entered the tent. As Moses went into the tent, the pillar of cloud would come down and stay at the entrance, while the LORD spoke with Moses. Whenever the people saw the pillar of cloud standing at the entrance to the tent, they all stood and worshiped, each at the entrance to his tent. The LORD would speak to Moses face to face, as a man speaks with his friend. Then Moses would return to the camp, but his young aide Joshua son of Nun did not leave the tent. (Exod. 33:7–11)

Moses set aside a special time and place to meet with God. The tent of meeting was for anyone who wanted to come into God's presence. The people took note of their leader's intimacy with God and were inspired by it. Being in the presence of God led to friendship with God.

Similarly, Joshua demonstrated a passionate hunger for the presence of God. Like Joshua, I want to cultivate a passion for God's presence in my life.

Gabriel had taught me that the key to epic faith was to find my way into the presence of God and to live my whole life there. Gabriel's words also taught me about being God's mouthpiece. Gabriel is known as the chief messenger angel. We too have been entrusted with God's message to share: the good news. Gabriel was given God's words to proclaim because he remained in God's presence.

Would I be faithful, then, with the message that God has given me? Another trip back to India would help me answer that question.

Living by Faith

IN early 2015 I traveled to India to teach for a school that equips young pioneers for new endeavors. I met six eager faces beaming back at me, ready to learn how to put God-given dreams into practice. During the week I shared many personal stories. I wanted to encourage these brave pioneers to believe great things of God and attempt great things for him. Although these young men and women from India and Nepal came from humble beginnings, when I heard about the dreams God had placed on their hearts, I knew I stood among future heroes of epic faith.

Tuangpu was a fiery young man from the tribal area of northeast India who had a vision to reach Burma for Jesus. Sita, a petite girl from north India, had a passion for the oppressed and felt called to advocate for justice. Ratan, a thoughtful young leader from south India, wanted to mobilize youth and plant Christian churches. Isaac, a powerful-looking young man from central India, demonstrated natural leadership potential. Finally, David and Pratik were best friends from Nepal:

David, a gifted evangelist with a passion to share the love of Jesus with anyone he met, and Pratik a worshiper who desired to lead others into the presence of God.

Like the dream seeds I spoke of in the previous chapter, I stood among potential sky-piercing giants. These men and women only needed a little encouragement to focus their faith and remain planted in the soil of God's presence to rise to their full potential.

During our week together, we studied the men and women from Hebrews 11, who are often referred to as the Faith Hall of Fame. Each one did great things for God "by faith." The writer of Hebrews speaks of their bold actions to bring glory to God. Faith emerges as the qualifying characteristic of their epic heroism.

On the morning of my last day of teaching, while praying, the Lord gave me an interesting assignment for class: "Marty, write Hebrews 11:41 and invite the students to do the same." Wondering what this meant, I opened my Bible but encountered a problem: the verse did not exist. Hebrews 11 concludes with verse 40.

> These were all commended for their faith, yet none of them received what had been promised. God had planned something better for us so that only together with us would they be made perfect. (Heb. 11:39–40)

The Lord showed me he was still writing this chapter through us. All these epic heroes did great things for God by faith—by believing that God resided with them and that he would work through them. The same is true for you and me as we trust that he will work through us. The recurring phrase throughout Hebrews 11 persists: "by faith."

Again, I heard the Shepherd's voice gently prodding me: "What will Marty do by faith? Write it down as a faith declaration."

I breathed a simple prayer and then wrote "Hebrews 11:41" as a heading in my journal. Then I penned these words:

> By faith, Marty and Kelly sold everything, left everything, and trusted that God would provide. By faith, they established missionary centers and equipped workers in pursuit of completing

the Great Commission. By faith, they received an abundant harvest for the King. By faith, the nations will be blessed through them.

When I finished writing this, I remembered the second part of the assignment: "Marty, write Hebrews 11:41 and invite the students to do the same." Jesus had prepared my day's lesson plan.

The students were already seated and ready to learn when I entered the small classroom. I instructed them to take out a blank sheet of paper and open their Bibles to Hebrews 11. We started by reading the entire chapter aloud. Then I asked, "What did these men and women do by faith?"

"Noah built an ark when there was no sign of rain," David stated.

"Moses was willing to choose a life of suffering with his people rather than a life of comfort as the Pharaoh's son," offered Isaac.

Sita commented, "Rahab protected the Israelite spies because she believed God was with them. It was because she took a risk of faith that Rahab and her whole family were spared."

"A study of these heroes' lives reveals that their faith was focused on God," I continued. "It's a faith based on the word of God, the voice of God, and the character of God. So how do the lives of the people we just read in Hebrews 11 demonstrate a faith based on the Word of God?"

"Moses was used by God to write the first five books of the Bible. These books, the word of God, became a pattern for the people of God to live by," Ratan stated.

"David wrote most of the Psalms, which are the word of God in song. It helped people worship God in spirit and truth," Pratik said.

"The people in Hebrews 11 did not have access to the complete Bible as we have today," I said. "But they knew God through the stories told by those who had gone before them. The people of God were careful to record what God had said, and what he had done, to inspire future generations to trust and obey him. Today, we often talk about knowing the Word of God, which is vitally important. But the people of Hebrews 11 encourage us to know God through the Word and to live accordingly. According to Hebrews 11, who would be an example of basing faith on the voice of God?"

They blurted out names from the list until Tuangpu interjected. "All of them followed the voice of God," he asserted.

"That is absolutely right. Let's focus on David. Over and over again in Scripture we see the phrase, 'David inquired of the Lord.' Whenever David needed to confront a problem or carry out an important decision, he would stop and ask for God's guidance. This distinguished David's life so markedly that I strongly believe it was the reason he was called a man after God's own heart. David loved God and desired to intimately follow his voice. Now let's talk about the faith of these heroes as it is focused on the character of God. On what aspects of God's character did they base their faith?" I asked.

"Enoch knew the presence of God," Pratik mentioned. "Enoch must have been one of the people who not only believed God existed, but would earnestly seek him."

"Abraham trusted God absolutely," Sita responded. "Abraham knew that God was faithful even when God asked him to sacrifice his son Isaac."

"That's right. Abraham didn't completely understand how God would work it all out, but he trusted him," I said. "He knew God was good and intended only the best. Abraham believed God could raise Isaac from the dead to fulfill the promise through him. Abraham reflects the character of another Father willing to sacrifice his only Son for a higher purpose, one who received that Son back from the grave."

I continued, "No wonder Abraham is called the father of faith. Basing our faith on the character of God is simply knowing God. When we have taken the time to know God relationally, we can trust him absolutely, and he will be able to trust us. Abraham made the list of the epic faithful because he trusted God and was willing to obey him. But I believe God is calling each of you to be men and women of epic faith too. God continues to write his story through you."

I asked students to take a blank sheet of paper and write "Hebrews 11:41" on the top and the words "By faith," followed by their name, on the next line. I explained, "This morning I felt that Jesus wanted each of us to write our own personal Hebrews 11:41. As a proclamation, record the great things that God will do through you." The moment seemed pregnant with faith. The silence in the room was broken by pens scribbling across sheets of paper—a beautiful sound.

When the silence returned I announced, "Now it's declaration time. Let's stand and read aloud the statements you have written." Feeling I should lead the way, I began to declare my personal Hebrews 11:41. One by one we announced our declarations with tears streaming down our faces.

Finally, David stood and read his statement. "Hebrews 11:41: By faith David traveled the world, reaching out with the gospel. He carried his cross in faithfulness and fulfilled the desire God had for him in the presence and favor of the Lord."

As students made their faith declarations, I felt like a proud father, especially of David. This was David, the orphaned boy we rescued in Nepal along with his sister, literally carrying them out of the Himalayas on our backs. This David, confidently making his faith declaration before me today, had once clung to my shoulders seventeen years earlier.

Kelly and I had become financial sponsors for David and his sister, Jasmine, and although we had kept in contact, we never had the opportunity to see them after our trek in Nepal. When David graduated from high school, he enrolled in a YWAM Discipleship Training School in India to become a missionary. We had raised the funds for him to attend, and then did so again for Jasmine when she also enrolled in a DTS.

After completing his discipleship school, David joined Youth With A Mission as a full-time missionary. Motivated to continue at the next level of training, he enrolled in our pioneering school in northern India. I was scheduled to teach at the school and was elated to finally reunite after so many years. When I arrived at the training center, David raced to meet me. As we were about to embrace in a manner typical of two grown men, he instead threw his arms around my waist like a little boy hugging his father—and would not let go. Overjoyed by our reunion, we spent the afternoon reminiscing and catching up.

"Uncle, I cannot believe I am actually seeing you after all this time," he beamed with the biggest smile, "I am just so happy."

At one point while conversing, David's tone grew serious. "Uncle, I remember one time as a boy when I wanted so badly to know from where I had come. I concentrated so hard to find my earliest memory. I thought maybe I could remember the village from where I came. But do you know what I remembered? I remember Auntie Kelly giving me my first bath. I was so little, but I remember her gently scrubbing all the dirt away. I could feel love as she poured warm water over me. That is my earliest memory."

Both our eyes were again moist and I couldn't fathom saying anything without falling apart.

"My second earliest memory is of you, Uncle. After my bath you returned from the market with new clothes for my sister and for me. You dressed me in grey sweat pants and a bright purple shirt with three smiling yaks on the front. You swooped me up on your shoulders and we all went out to the market with me riding high and Auntie holding Jasmine."

"I have a surprise for you, David," I announced as I wiped my face with the tail of my shirt. Before I had left, Kelly and I had combed through our old photo albums for pictures from that very trip and prepared a small album containing photographs David had never seen. I presented David with the gift; he stared at each image as through a window of his early life history.

"I have never seen pictures like this. Look how little we were when we were carried from Tattopani over the pass. You even have pictures of my first bath! And there is my purple yak shirt. Look how I could ride on your shoulders then, Uncle."

Sending an occasional letter and a check every month for the past seventeen years had stretched Kelly and me. Each contribution was an act of faith. But until that day, I had failed to see our profound impact on two precious lives on the other side of the world. Our financial support and involvement seemed insignificant at times, but for David and Jasmine we were heroes of faith who helped shape the course of their lives.

As David and I shared stories I realized we were both living testimonies of Hebrews 11:41.

"Uncle, did you know that I had to return to the village of my birth to document my identity so that I could get a passport?" David asked. It is not uncommon for those born in remote areas of India and Nepal to lack a birth certificate or any official document of identity. Many do not know their own birthday or even their age.

I was intrigued. "What happened?"

"I wanted to attend the DTS in Bangalore, India, but to go out of Nepal I needed a passport. I knew I could not get a passport without official papers, so when I was eighteen years old I made a journey to the village where I came from."

While there, he learned the hard truth about his mother and father and what the Lord had rescued him from.

"Uncle, I found out my father was a drunkard, a violent man. Everyone in my whole village feared him. They told me my father died by vomiting blood. It was very sad to hear these things. Mother died by falling off a cliff, but my relatives told me it was more likely a suicide. When I visited my village, I realized Jesus had rescued me from ending up like my mother and father."

The grandmother who cared for David and Jasmine did the best she could but approached our team that day to take them away because she was afraid she was dying and that the children would be sold into slavery. David had held no hope of ever meeting this grandmother, presuming her to be dead, but when he returned to his village after fourteen years to obtain birth documents, he discovered that his grandmother was still alive. When she saw David for the first time, she began to scream his father's name in absolute horror. Apparently David looked just like his father, and in her confusion his grandmother thought his father had come back from the dead.

"No, Grandmother, it's me, David, my father's son," David told her. When she realized who David was, she embraced him and kissed him, overjoyed to see him again after all those years.

"The people in my village wondered what had happened to us. They thought two small children taken by the white people had certainly been abused and mistreated. But I told them my sister and I were loved and cared for. I also told them about the Creator God who loved and cared for us too. Uncle, when I told them about Jesus, the entire village listened as if I was an angel sent from God."

IRONICALLY, right now as this chapter is being written, David is once again making a trip back to the village of his birth, this time with his sister Jasmine. David recently e-mailed Kelly and me:

Dear Uncle and Auntie,

When we left the village I was nearly about five years old but now I am twenty-three. Jasmine was nearly two years old and now she is going to be twenty this month.

Uncle, I am so thankful to you and Auntie for coming to our village and obeying God's voice. Because you took us from there we got to know Jesus as our Savior.

For our whole life our relatives have treated us like strangers. They never even visited us or bothered about me and Jasmine, but I deeply feel that we should go and preach God's love and gospel to them. Uncle, you went to my village eighteen years back to share the gospel and now we want to go and share God's love. Please do pray for the journey ahead.

With lots of love,

David and Jasmine

Because Kelly and I took simple steps of faith, David and Jasmine clearly saw the compassion of God demonstrated through our lives. When we are used by God to live out epic faith, we will naturally reflect the character of God. David and Jasmine came to know God as a loving Father as they experienced the care, provision, protection, and affirmation of their adoptive parents, John and Elizabeth, and other faithful followers of God.

These stories demonstrate that Hebrews 11:41 has already been fulfilled repeatedly in our lives via faith. We pray that God will inspire many others toward the same epic faith that has motivated us.

Afterword

I WHOLEHEARTEDLY believe that God is calling each person who reads this book to become a man or woman of epic faith. God is still writing his story through you, so now it is your turn.

I encourage you to read Hebrews 11 and then write your own Hebrews 11:41 statement. Begin a daily venture living out your own epic faith story.

Focus on God and live according to his Word.

Hear and follow his voice.

Pray big prayers and believe God for great things. He is a great God; he will always act in ways consistent with his character.

The world is in desperate need of the Father's love and needs you to show what that looks like. Continue to live in epic faith by following the Word of God, hearing his voice, and reflecting God's character as you walk in obedience.

If this book has been a blessing and you have seen God working in your life by practicing *Epic Faith* principles, then please visit www.epic-faith.net and share your story. This website will allow you to record your own testimony to encourage others. You can also order the workbook, *30 Days of Epic Faith*, and find free downloads to inspire your continued walk of faith. Additionally, you will find suggestions for starting an *Epic Faith* study group within your church or community. Let us work together to ignite an epic movement of loving Jesus and living by faith.

Epic Next Steps

IT'S time to take the next steps of your own epic faith journey. Use this page as a checklist to complete as many steps as possible in the next twelve months.

- ☐ Order and work through the *30 Days of Epic Faith* workbook: www.epicfaith.net.
- ☐ Develop a plan for your personal daily time with God in his Word.
- ☐ Challenge your faith by reading a biography from the Christian Heroes: Then & Now series by Janet and Geoff Benge: www.ywampublishing.com.
- ☐ Use the gifts that God has given you by volunteering in your church or community.
- ☐ Pray daily for three friends or family members who do not know Jesus personally. Then create opportunities to share your faith with them.
- ☐ Attend an *Epic Faith* retreat: www.epicfaith.net.
- ☐ Write out your God-sized dream and take steps toward accomplishing it.
- ☐ Do a Mission Adventure or Discipleship Training School with Youth With A Mission: www.ywamidaho.org.
- ☐ Care for children like David and Jasmine through the ministry of Streams of Mercy: www.streamsofmercy.org.
- ☐ Set an alarm for 9:37 a.m. as a reminder to pray daily that Jesus will send workers for the harvest according to Matthew 9:37–38.
- ☐ Support an indigenous church planter in India or Nepal: www.harvestfrontiers.org.
- ☐ Start an *Epic Faith* study group within your church or community: www.epicfaith.net.
- ☐ Consider how Jesus is calling you to engage in his mission: www.ywam.org.